Liverpool banks & bankers, 1760-1837

A history of the circumstances which gave rise to the industry, and of the men who founded and developed it

John Hughes

Alpha Editions

This edition published in 2020

ISBN : 9789390400515 (Hardback)
ISBN : 9789390400676 (Paperback)

Design and Setting By
Alpha Editions
www.alphaedis.com
email - alphaedis@gmail.com

PREFACE

In compiling this work my aim has been to give, briefly but clearly, a connected account of the origin and progress of all the private banks of Liverpool, to show who and what were the several partners, and to give short accounts of their family relations. It is an attempt to place on record succinct biographical notices, not to be found in such completeness elsewhere, of Liverpool bankers. The materials have been garnered, after long and patient quest, from numerous sources. The most fertile source has been the newspapers of the period, of which in all about one hundred years have been studied. And to the advertisements in no small measure am I indebted for facts which have illumined the gloom in which the history of Liverpool banking rested. But the very spirit of the times precluded the newspapers from being other than exceedingly cautious in

their accounts of men and events. The severity
of the laws of libel induced extreme reticence.
Hence much of real interest in the history of the
banks has been for ever sealed from us.

During the middle of the eighteenth century,
when the commerce of Liverpool was rapidly
expanding, it is somewhat surprising to find no
established banks. Yet at that period there was
a similar state of affairs throughout England.
Mr. Hylton Price states that in 1750 there were
not more than twelve banks established out of
London. Yet, and especially in a busy commercial town like Liverpool, banking business
had to be done, bills had to be negotiated,
some one had to perform the function of a
banker though not specifically known by the
name. Hence arose a class of man, trader or
merchant, who acted as bankers to the community,
still retaining a separate business. The date 1760
is not an exact, but a convenient, date to indicate
the period of the rise of bankers. From the very
nature of the process of evolution no precise date
can be assigned. This is a point I wish to make

clear : that in the case of all the early bankers there was no definite period at which it can be said that banking commenced. No bank came into existence as such all at once. In all the cases of the earliest banks there was gradual growth, side by side with the merchant's or trader's business, until ultimately one or the other became dominant. If the banking side became stronger, the bank made its public appearance. This being so, we need not look for palatial buildings, nor for costly interiors, in the early banks. Rather let us look for the merchant's counting-house or the tradesman's back parlour, with limited accessories — in the extreme case a plain deal table. It is on record that Mr. Lewis Loyd, who established the famous bank of Jones, Loyd & Co. of Lothbury, E.C., ever kept in his bedroom the small table on which his first banking transactions were done in his shop at Manchester.

But it is evident that force of character and special aptitudes were the prime factors in determining the success or otherwise of the venture.

The seed laid in good ground produced mighty trees, whilst that which fell in stony ground sprang up rapidly, and as rapidly withered away.

As this work is entirely a personal effort, one which has its sole basis in my own research, it doubtless follows that there are errors of omission and commission. I am in sincere hopes that the latter are but few and inconsiderable, and trust that my business training has succeeded in ensuring the desirable accuracy of dates. As to errors of omission, I have done what I could to avoid these. But there must be in possession of local families much interesting material bearing on the private side of banking in the early periods, and I would take it as a courteous act if any reader, having knowledge of such, would kindly communicate with me.

For the rest, I desire to return my heartfelt thanks for the willing assistance given me through many years by Mr. Peter Cowell and his assistants, Messrs. Henry E. Curran, Charles Robertson,

George M. Parry, and F. J. Waters, of the
William Brown Street Library. In recent years
Mr. George T. Shaw, Master and Librarian of
the Athenæum, has been unfailingly helpful. To
John Naylor, Esq., I am indebted for his critical
supervision of the chapter on Leyland and
Bullins. Messrs. Henry Young & Sons and
myself are grateful for the ready assistance
afforded in obtaining portraits and views by
Mrs. Henry Bright; Mrs. Heywood Bright;
Mrs. G. W. Moss; John Naylor, Esq.; Alfred
Holt, Esq.; C. E. Hope, Esq.; Arthur Hey-
wood, Esq.; J. Hope Simpson, Esq., and J. C.
M. Jacobs, Esq., of the Bank of Liverpool, and
the Directorate of the said bank; the Direc-
torate of the London City and Midland Bank;
the Committee of the Athenæum; A. W.
Stanyforth, Esq.; Edward P. Thompson, Esq.;
Henry Yates Thompson, Esq.; R. Stewart-
Brown, Esq.; and Mr. G. F. Graham.

In the majority of instances the portraits
and views have never before been reproduced,
and, being authentic illustrations of people and

places of great importance in the history of Liverpool, they possess an interest and value which it is difficult to overestimate.

To my sense of local patriotism is due the present volume, which it is hoped may help to an understanding of one of the forces which have contributed to the building up of my native city of Liverpool.

To my own case apply the words of Izaak Walton: "And however it appeals to him, yet I am sure I have found a high content in the search and conference of what is here offered to the Reader's view and censure; I wish him as much in the perusal of it."

JOHN HUGHES.

280 Kensington,
Liverpool, *November* 1905.

CONTENTS

CHAPTER VI

CHAPTER VII

CHAPTER VIII

CHAPTER IX

CHAPTER X

CHAPTER XI

CHAPTER XII

CONTENTS

CHAPTER XIII

CHAPTER XIV

CHAPTER XV

CHAPTER XVI

CHAPTER XVII

CHAPTER XVIII

CHAPTER XIX

LIST OF PLATES

View of—

Facsimile of—

CHAPTER I

BRIEF VIEW OF LIVERPOOL AND ITS COMMERCE.

The references to bankers in histories of Liverpool—Ships and commerce of eighteenth century—Shipping trades, foreign and home —East India Company — Roads and stage-coaches — Canals— Streets — Lighting — Water — Numeration of houses—Curious trades.

WHEN Samuel Derrick, Master of the Ceremonies at Bath, visited Liverpool in 1760, he found that he had "nowhere met with any account of the very opulent town," and lest his friend the Earl of Cork should be equally in ignorance, he proceeded forthwith to remedy the defect.

So the author, surveying the now numerous records of the annals of his native town, finds that no connected account of the early Banks of Liverpool has yet appeared. The earliest historian, Enfield (1773), does not mention them, nor does Wallace (1795) nor Troughton (1810); Smithers (1830) has but scanty reference to them, and Baines (1852), Brooke (1853), and even Picton (1873) have very sparse accounts. Yet few will gainsay that there is an exceedingly close connection between the growth of

A

commerce and the growth of one of its chief
instruments.

The first Liverpool Directory was published in
1766, and therein no banker is mentioned. In
the Directory of 1774 we find in the body of
the work "William Clarke, banker and linen
draper, 34, Castle Street," and in the appendix
" C. Caldwell & Co., banker's office, 37, Paradise
Street."

When Samuel Derrick wrote there was a vast
difference between the Liverpool he described
and the Liverpool of to-day. Could the inhabitants of that date revisit the glimpses of the
moon, their astonishment would be great at the
wondrous developments in the size, population,
and trade of the good town of Liverpool. For
they were then proud, and justly proud, of the
increasing wealth and importance of their town,
brought about by the enterprise of its merchants
and seamen. Consider that steam-power was
not, that the leviathans of modern commerce
were beyond the dreams of the most sanguine,
yet that long voyages were conducted in what
we should now deem the veriest cockle-shells of
boats. The average tonnage in 1773 was but
110 tons, and thirty years later the average had
risen only to 240. Yet these comparatively tiny
barks were employed on round voyages of six
to twelve months' duration. Moreover, onwards

from 1776, when war was declared with America,
followed in 1778 by war with France, in 1780
with Spain and Holland, they had to contend
with the dangers of ships of war and privateers
in addition to the ordinary perils of the sea.
Pluck, perseverance, fertility of resource, and
thorough practical seamanship were essential to
the business, and with the aid of these, the commercial status of Liverpool was attained and
sustained. The principal trades of Liverpool
were the African and West Indian, but large
supplementary business was done with the Baltic,
salt principally being exported, and a progressive
trade was carried on with America. This was
of course impeded by the unhappy war with the
Colonies, but after the recognition of the independence of the United States it soon recovered.
The trade with Ireland was also very large, and
considerable business was done in the Mediter-
ranean Sea. As yet the monopoly which the
East India Company possessed in the trade with
the East Indies and China had not been abro-
gated. A public meeting on the subject was
held in Liverpool in 1792, and as a result Dr.
James Currie drew up a petition to Government
praying that the monopoly should cease. The
memorable commercial distress of the following
year retarded the advance of the movement, and
not till 1813 was there a partial relaxation of

the monopoly. This was followed by additional relief in 1834, but not till 1849 was there a complete sweeping away of the uncontrolled sway of John Company. When William Roscoe was Member of Parliament for Liverpool he, on 23rd February 1807, spoke in the House of Commons on the Abolition of Slavery Bill, and whilst supporting the Bill remarked on the wider spheres of commerce which would compensate England for the loss of the nefarious traffic, and incidentally protested against the monopoly of the East India Company. "Let there," said he, amidst applause from all sides of the House—"let there be no monopoly but the monopoly of the country at large."

Prior to 1760 there was no coach-road nearer to Liverpool than Warrington. In that year, however, a road was made practicable for coaches, and thus Liverpool was connected with the other towns of the kingdom. Before this all travelling had to be done on horseback, and such luggage and merchandise as was sent by land was transported on pack-horses, and for many years later, until 1785, pack-horses were employed to carry His Majesty's mails. When this coach-road to Warrington was constructed, stage-coaches began to run between Liverpool and London (May 1760), and Liverpool and Manchester (September 1760). The house of

call in Liverpool for the former was the "Golden
Talbot" in Water Street. The Bank of Liverpool
now occupies its site. It was then kept by Mrs.
Rathbone. The Manchester coach put up at the
"Golden Fleece," on the north side of Dale Street.
It was then kept by Thomas Banner, the ancestor
of Mr. J. S. Harmood Banner.[1]

The growth of traffic thereafter rapidly increased, and the coaching business to and from
Liverpool attained large proportions. But from
the Manchester district the greater part of the
goods came round by canals, which were commenced in 1720, and gradually became numerous
and important. The first real canal in England
(*i.e.* a cutting of the water-way through solid
earth) was the Sankey Canal, commenced in
1755,[2] which joins the Mersey at Fiddler's
Ferry. Before this, so-called canals were only
improvements of the natural water-way.

From 1760 to the close of the eighteenth
century the town was of very small extent.
Castle Street was one of the principal streets,
then as now, but it was not more than eighteen
feet wide. In this street, and Redcross Street,

[1] Mr. Thomas Banner died at Richmond (Liverpool) on 6th July
1807, aged 85, "revered by his family and respected by all who knew
him."
[2] This canal was completed 9th January 1758. It was projected
and executed by Henry Berry, who died at his house in Duke Street,
Liverpool, on 30th July 1812, aged 92.

were the fashionable shops. All the streets were exceedingly narrow; in addition, they were dirty and ill-paved, and all the principal streets had to undergo the costly and troublesome process of widening. Castle Street was widened in 1786–7, and Dale Street in 1807–8. The latter street was the main entrance into Liverpool, and in it, with the increase of coaching, all the various industries dependent thereon waxed and flourished. Hotels, inns, eating-houses, saddlers, blacksmiths, &c., were numerous. Vast stables, some of them capable of putting up 100 horses, were attached to the hotels and coaching establishments.

Lord Street was a very narrow street, and was shut out from its present opening. The houses of Castle Street ran along to Cable Street, and entrance to Lord Street was to be had only by way of Castle Ditch, one end of which opened into Harrington Street, the other into Cable Street. In 1826 Lord Street was widened to the extent of four times its original size,[1] and the present noble entrance was provided by the construction of the Crescent.

Pool Lane (now South Castle Street) is a very

---

[1] It is noteworthy that on the occasion of the laying of the first line of improvement on 12th July 1826 the tenant of the then No. 80, Mr. John Orrell, a saddler, sufficiently recognised the real import of the coming change by providing a cold repast and cold punch for about 100 persons, in order that the function should be properly celebrated.

ancient street. As the name indicates, it led to the cradle of Liverpool's commercial greatness, the Pool of Liverpool, which was, under the Act 8 Anne, c. 12, converted into the first dock in England. In 1811 the Dock Trust obtained powers to close the Old Dock, and to erect a custom-house and other buildings on the site. But this was not put into effect for several years, and not till September 1826 was a start made by clearing the dock of all shipping. The other streets converging on this centre of commerce, Duke Street and Hanover Street, were important streets. In them, many of the men whose enterprise gave Liverpool the opportunity of becoming what it is resided; for these streets were high-class residential streets, the merchant himself being in possession, whilst his counting-house and warehouses were at the back of the dwelling-house.

Church Street, from 1760 to practically the close of the century, was entirely a residential street. Bold Street was commenced to be laid out in 1786, and was also a residential street. Ranelagh Street, Brownlow Hill, and Mount Pleasant had a few houses in them. Park Lane was in existence, and in Great George Street building was commenced in 1785. But all the land lying between Church Street and Berry Street, and between Duke Street and Park Lane, was not

built on till later. The population of Toxteth
Park was but scant and scattered, and taking the
town in another direction we find so late as 1807
"Bevington Lodge for sale, one mile from Liverpool Exchange, with an extensive garden of fruit-
trees, faces Everton Hill, and the back overlooks
the Mersey." Much later, in 1839, Everton itself
is described as the "rural retreat of commercial
opulence."

Till towards the close of the eighteenth century
the district north of Tithebarn Street was open
country. Near the foot of the present Richmond
Row the stream from the Moss Lake entered
through the present Downe Street, and clustered
on either side of the stream were the kennels of
the Liverpool Hound Hunt, a pack of harriers
to which the Corporation was a subscriber. But
Liverpool was behind other large towns in much
regarding its streets. As before stated, they were
narrow, dirty, and ill-paved. Moreover, they
had no side-walks, or parapets as they were, and
are, locally called. So late as 1799 we have such
a picture as this: "The spirited and laudable
example set the town by the owners and occupiers
of houses and shops in Lord Street in flagging
the footwalks opposite their premises will, we hope,
be speedily followed. . . . It is an improvement
accomplished in every other principal city and town
in the kingdom." Even when this was done

the inhabitants were not too careful to keep them clean. In 1802 about seventy of the principal inhabitants of Castle Street, Lord Street, Church Street, and Pool Lane were fined 5s. each by the Mayor for not sweeping and cleansing the parapet walks before their houses, shops, &c.

The town was lighted by oil-lamps, and as this was done by contract, it was not too well done, and many were the collisions between the authorities and the contractors on this score. Not till 1819 was Castle Street lighted with gas.

Water was obtained from wells, the sandstone formation yielding a very fair supply. Those inhabitants who had not these conveniences were supplied from huge barrels mounted on wheels, drawn by a horse, at so much per bucket, or hessian, or "heshin," as it was locally called. In the drawing by Herdman, depicting the burning of the Town Hall in 1795, two of these tanks are shown with their accompanying hessians. The price in 1765 was four pails full for a penny. In their Improvement Act of 1786 the Corporation took power to supply the inhabitants with water from the wells. But nothing was done in the matter until a company obtained powers, under the Act 39 Geo. III. c. 36, to revive the powers which Sir Cleave Moore had obtained in 8 Anne, c. 25, "to bring water into Liverpool from the Bootle springs." Then the Corporation

formed a company of their own, the subscription
for which was immediately taken up, and made
over to it the powers acquired in 1786. Both
companies then set to work, and supplied the
town through wooden pipes, afterwards replaced
by iron. Some of these wooden pipes are
occasionally met with in digging foundations.

The numeration of the houses was very unsatisfactory, and occasioned much tribulation
to good John Gore in the compilation of his
directories. There is a certain grim humour on
the title-page of the directories of 1796 and
1800: "With the *Numbers* as they are (*or ought
to be*) affixed to their houses."

The system employed was that the numeration
commenced on the left side of a street and continued consecutively to the bottom, and then
turned up on the other side. Thus in a finished
street the first number and the last number
would face each other. Take a familiar street,
Dale Street. In 1818 George Forwood had an
office at 2 Dale Street, and immediately opposite
was the bank of Messrs. Moss, Dale, Rogers,
and Moss, No. 179. Until matters were settled
there was sometimes a doubt as to which end
of a street the numeration commenced. For
instance, in the case of Castle Street, in 1793,
the advertisements in the papers reverse the
order in which the directory places them. The

latter commenced at the Dale Street end, the former at that of James Street. This consecutive method of numeration was in use till 1838–9. The directory for 1839 employs for the first time the alternate mode of numeration. In this connection it is worthy of note that in many of the old-established streets of London the old method is still used. The Strand is a familiar example.

With reference to the description of the inhabitants, as given in the directory and elsewhere, we find several curiosities. Anybody above "the rank of a shopkeeper" (to misquote W. S. Gilbert) is styled a merchant; and be it noted that the place where the latter did his business was a "counting - house," while a mere broker or attorney employed an "office" for his work. A note on the gradual putting forward of the dining hour will be found in a subsequent chapter.

We have some quaint trades mentioned in our old Liverpool, of which "leather breeches maker," for example, has gone with the post-boy and the changed mode of travelling.

With increased knowledge and application of science the "dealer in leeches" and "bleeder with leeches" have gone as distinctive trades. I regret the disappearance of the "stocking grafter," illustrating so well the story of the old lady who boasted she had worn one pair of stockings for thirty years, renewing the foot or leg portion as required. The "money scrivener" has disappeared in name only, but the "corn meter" has gone for ever. Changed conditions of shipping have submerged the "broker for the flats," but, had he a monopoly, what a business he would enjoy to-day on the Liverpool Cotton, Corn, and Stock Exchanges.

CHAPTER II

GENERAL VIEW OF FINANCIAL HISTORY FROM
1760, WITH SPECIAL REFERENCE TO LIVER-
POOL.

Rise of manufacturing processes—French Revolution of 1793—Bank
Restriction Act—Increase of country banks—National Debt—
Profits of Bank of England and Bank of Ireland—Consols—Commercial distress—Peace of 1814 and 1815, and consequent effect
on prices—First issue of sovereigns and half-sovereigns—Partial
resumption of cash payments—Scaling down of interest on loans
—Large issue of paper money—Speculations of 1824 and 1825,
and consequent grave crisis—Great stoppage of banks—Establishment of branches of Bank of England—Commencement of joint-
stock banks — Stamp duties — Liverpool joint-stock banks—
Gradual supersession of private banks.

THE latter part of the eighteenth century and
the commencement of the nineteenth mark the
period when manufactures and commerce parted
from the old and embarked into the new methods,
which have resulted in the enormous expansion
of modern times. It was an inventive age, and
the year 1767, when Hargreaves invented the
spinning-jenny, was the starting-point of successive additions to the mechanical substitutes
for the slow processes of hand labour. This improvement was followed in 1769 by Arkwright

taking out his first patent for spinning with
rollers. In 1774 the Rev. Dr. Cartwright
patented his invention of the power-loom, and
in 1776 the mule was invented by Samuel
Crompton. Then followed the application of
steam-power. Watt in 1782 made himself illus-
trious by the patent of the perfected steam-
engine. Many improvements followed, until
Robert Fulton in America had the satisfaction
of seeing his paddle-steamers on the Hudson
from 1806 onwards. The first steamboat on the
Mersey arrived in May 1815, having been built
to ply between Liverpool and Runcorn.

Liverpool was the chief port for the output
of the improved processes, and greatly benefited
thereby. But the progress was impeded by the
various wars from 1776 onwards. When peace
seemed established, and commerce was rapidly increasing, came the war of the French Revolution.
On the declaration of war in 1793 there was
a panic throughout the country. Hundreds of
commercial houses became bankrupt, and about
seventy country bankers stopped payment: one-
third of the number then existing. In Liverpool,
Charles Caldwell & Co. became bankrupt, and
Gregson & Co. had to have their affairs looked
into, but survived the ordeal. In this connection Dr. James Currie writes under date
16th March 1793: "The first merchant in

Liverpool has failed, and many others must
follow. Private credit is entirely at a stand."
In this extremity the Corporation of Liverpool,
on behalf of the town, sought aid from the Bank
of England, but were refused it. They then
obtained a special Act of Parliament enabling
them to issue promissory notes against produce.
This had the effect of relieving the distress.
A detailed account of this unique transaction
appears in a subsequent chapter. The Government introduced a special Bill for temporary
advances on the credit of the country, having the
same intentions, and under the Act 332 persons
made application for advances to the amount of
£3,855,624. Of these 238 were granted to the
extent of £2,202,200.

Gold, which was so much required for the purposes of war, became scarce, and the drain on the
Bank became so excessive that by 25th February
1797 the stock of gold was only £1,270,000. Then
came the Bank Restriction Act. It was originally
stated that the restriction was to last for fifty-two
days only, but, with brief intervals, it lasted till
1825. When the payment of cash for notes was
not compulsory came the great increase in the
number of private bankers, all paper issuing. They
increased in eight years from 230 to 517, and the
increase went on until, in the year 1814, there
were no less than 940. The panic of 1815–16

wiped out so many that at the end of the latter
year there were only 752, and further depletions,
culminating in the *débâcle* of 1825, reduced the
number to 552. Thus in eleven years about 400
so-called banks became bankrupt.

In the meantime the requirements of the
Government were such that the National Debt
went up by leaps and bounds. Each successive
year saw a fresh loan, until from £260,000,000
in 1793, the National Debt reached the colossal
figure of £895,000,000 in 1816. In the words
of a sprightly writer: "During the war of the
French Revolution . . . the Bank of England,
unrestrained by a liability to pay in specie, diffused
its notes with a prodigal hand; and every man
who could get a bill accepted could get it cashed.
. . . The Minister had hundreds of millions to
borrow in loans, and tens of millions to raise in
revenue; and loans could not be raised and taxes
paid unless trade was lively and the circulation
full and free; and accordingly, when the Prime
Minister winked his eye, the Bank governor
nodded his head, and bank-notes were dealt out
like cards at a gambling table; every man who
could give an IOU to the marker being at
perfect liberty to play the game he pleased, and
take his chance of ruin in the general sport."

Hence of Pitt it was said, *Auream invenit,
chartaceam relinquet.*

Through the inflation of their respective issues
the Bank of England in nineteen years made a
profit of £29,280,636 on a capital of £11,642,000,
and the Bank of Ireland a profit of £11,361,650
on a capital of £3,000,000.

In such a state of affairs it was only too probable that there must be violent fluctuations in
the price of commodities. Consols in 1797 fell
as low as 47½, and in 1798 to 47¼, the highest
point reached in the latter year being 58.

In this connection Dr. James Currie writes,
under date February 22, 1797: "Orders have
been sent up to London to sell (Funds) without
restriction to a great amount. . . . In consequence
of this a principal banker told me that money had
flowed back on him so much that he was absolutely at a loss what to do with it; as he, for his
own part, would not purchase another sixpence in
the Funds, and could not lend it out on commercial adventure in the present state of things.
Thus large sums are beginning to rest in the
bankers' hands without the power of converting
them to account."

But very shortly there was the swing of the
pendulum in the opposite direction. Liverpool
was hardly pressed in 1799, and an Act had to
be passed, "an Act for enabling His Majesty to
direct the issue of Exchequer Bills to a limited
amount, and in the manner therein mentioned,

for the relief of the merchants of Liverpool and Lancaster." Commissioners were appointed, and an office opened in Water Street for the purpose. Banking matters in Liverpool appeared to go on smoothly. Certainly an ephemeral bank, Sir Michael Cromie, Pownoll, & Hartman, disappeared in 1801, but nothing of moment occurred till 1807. That year witnessed the accession to the list of bankers of Moss & Co. and Joseph Hadwen. Thomas Leyland also separated himself from Clarke & Roscoe, and commenced the firm of Leyland & Bullin. Gregson & Co. and Richard Hanly both suspended payment. But the close of 1809 and the whole of 1810 witnessed great commercial distress. There was so great a fall in prices and destruction of private credit as was then without precedent. It is said that half the traders in the kingdom became bankrupt, and it is certain that Liverpool had its share.

When on Friday, 20th July 1810, the settling day for Consols on the London Stock Exchange, it was found there was no one to receive the Stocks bought, there was an alarming shock to mercantile confidence. The Government loan for that year, £14,000,000, had been taken by two firms, Baring & Co. and Goldschmidt & Co. The Stocks suddenly fell to a discount. Panic ensued, and the discount was as much as

6 per cent. Sir F. Baring had died, and Goldschmidt took his losses so much to heart that
he shot himself.

The loss of confidence and consequent panic
arose out of the speculative dealings with the
American possessions of Spain and Portugal,
which in 1808 had been thrown open to direct
trade with England. Vast amounts of English
manufactures had been sent abroad in 1808
and 1809, and caused an inflation of prices
in England. After a while it was seen there
was no return for the vast exports. And small
wonder, in many cases. Goods, sent specu-
latively to places where there were few or no
warehouses, had to lie on the beach; and discri-
mination was not shown, for stoves and hearth-
rugs were sent to Buenos Aires! Then came
the fall in prices, and panic took possession of
the whole trading community, and extensive embarrassments resulted.

Billinge's *Liverpool Advertiser* for 13th August
1810 has an admirable leaderette :—

"It is lamentable to observe the wantonness with
which men speak of the credit of the most eminent
houses, in consequence of the recent distresses in the
commercial world. Talk of gossiping at the tea-table !
The tongues of antiquated maidens are not more loose,
nor their insinuations more scandalous, than those of
some gossiping men ; and when it is considered that

credit is to a merchant what chastity is to a woman, this licentious practice of whispering away reputation cannot be too severely condemned."

Early in 1811 the Government found it necessary to introduce a " Commercial Credit " Bill, to enable traders to obtain means to finance their holdings of produce. The second reading of the Bill took place on 16th March, and on the previous day a meeting of the principal merchants, brokers, and traders was convened at the Liverpool Town Hall to take into consideration the expediency of an application to Government for a participation in the loan of Exchequer Bills " now about to be issued for the relief of commerce." The resolution declared that this town, from the peculiar nature, extent, and importance of its commerce, was in a situation to require, and was entitled to expect, a participation in the public aid now about to be offered to the trading part of the nation ; and that it was highly expedient that a respectful application to that effect should be made to Government without delay.

The third reading of the Bill was carried by 41 to 4, and on 8th April an office was opened in the Exchange for the Commissioners for the issue of Exchequer Bills.

The question of the monopoly of the East India Company as to the trade with India and

China was constantly occupying the minds of every business community in England, and Liverpool naturally wished to share in that Eastern trade.   On 17th March 1812 a meeting of merchants, &c., took place in the Town Hall to take into consideration the propriety of petitioning Parliament for the wished-for participation. When partial relief came in 1813, Mr. John Gladstone was one of the first to avail himself of the opportunities offered.

In 1813 John and James Aspinall relinquished their tea, &c., business and became bankers solely, under the title of John Aspinall & Son.

Though matters on the surface seemed fairly prosperous, yet there was a deep internal unrest. The gulf between the nominal and the actual value of Bank of England paper was yearly widening (see Chap. III.), and thus prices were become more and more inflated.

The advent of peace in 1814, and the subsequent entire cessation of war in 1815, pricked the bubble.   Prices then tumbled on all sides.   During the war, every manufacture was stimulated. Copper, tin, lead, and iron were all required, and were extensively mined for.   As a consequence, coals were in demand.   There was need for large quantities of farm produce.   Thus enclosures of common lands were made on a vast scale.   From 1795 to 1815 no less than 1798 Enclosure Bills passed the House of Commons, and from 1790 to 1820 no less than 3,965,270 acres passed from communal to private hands. Those who would refrain from stealing the goose from the common did not scruple to steal the common from the goose. With the cessation of war came glutted markets; for demand stopped, whilst production went on. Shipping correspondingly suffered. For commerce the result was naturally disastrous, and a great wave of ruin swept over the country. It was felt till well on in 1816, and during the two years 1815 and 1816, 240 banking firms either partially suspended business or became bankrupt.

Locally, the banking firms of Roscoe, Clarke, & Roscoe, and John Aspinall & Son, were involved. The former held out hopes of a surplus, and was put in train for liquidation, but the latter entirely succumbed. In September 1816 a town's meeting was summoned by the Mayor, to take into consideration the distresses of the country and the best means to be adopted for remedying the same. The condition of the country was indeed grievous, so much so that the intended resumption of cash payments was entirely prevented. It was then intended to call in all £1 and £2 notes.

The following year saw the change in the coinage. The *Gazette* for 8th July 1817 contains the particulars of the new sovereigns and

half - sovereigns which were to supplant the
existing gold coinage. Vast amounts of gold
were coined, but the failure of the harvest in
1818 necessitated its exportation in payment for
imported corn. The total amount so expended
was £7,000,000. In 1818 there was a further
addition to the silver coinage of £3,000,000,
principally in crowns.

The year 1819 was also exceedingly bad for
the commerce of the country. A correspondent
in Gore's *Advertiser* in April gives a very gloomy
picture of Liverpool: "Commerce was never in
such a state as at present, property of every kind
depreciating daily. Holders of colonial produce
generally, and of cotton especially, are particularly
hard hit. The recent failures will produce most
disastrous results, not only directly, but indirectly,
by the destruction of confidence." He therefore
appeals to the merchants of Liverpool to apply
at once for a grant of Exchequer Bills from
Government.

But Government could do nothing. They
were at their wits' end for money. The Bank
of England had contracted its issues, a panic
ensued, and a rush for gold was made of such
severity that on 5th April 1819 Parliament
hurried through a Bill restricting the Bank of
England from paying their notes in cash. Want
and discontent pervaded the kingdom. Allusion

only is necessary in these pages to the "Battle
of Peterloo" on 16th July in this year. The
year 1822 was next fixed for the resumption
of cash payments, and the Bank of England
advertised that they would remit any amount of
gold coin of the realm in sums not less than
£3000 on application to the chief cashier
prior to 1st February, extended afterwards to
1st March, and again to 1st April. But the
depression in the country was so great that
the scheme had further to be postponed, and
an Act of Parliament was passed authorising
the issue of country bankers' small notes until
5th January 1833, the year of the expiry of
the Bank of England's charter.

In the following year, 1823, rates of interest
began to droop, and in 1824 Government scaled
down its Four per Cents. to 3½ per cent.

In Liverpool the banks gave notice that on and
after 1st January 1824 it was their intention to
calculate interest and discount approved bills at
the reduced rate of 4 per cent. There would
naturally be a corresponding reduction in the
interest allowed on deposits. The Bank of
Scotland, whose rate of interest on deposits was
4 per cent. in 1822, reduced it in 1823 to 3 per
cent., and in 1824 to 2 per cent.

Having no longer the fear of extinction before
their eyes, the country bankers, who had largely

restricted their issues, now expanded them to the
fullest extent, and the Bank of England issued
its notes against its large stock of gold. Lord
Liverpool stated in the House that the amount
of country bankers' notes stamped in 1821, 1822,
and 1823 had been on an average a little above
four millions. In 1824 it reached six millions,
and in 1825 exceeded eight millions. The low-
ness of interest obtainable, and the plethora of
circulation, fostered speculation, and speculation
became rampant both in foreign and home
concerns.

In 1823 had begun a series of loans to foreign
nations, principally to the newly recognised South
American Republics and Brazil, and in the three
years 1823–4–5 no less than £56,000,000 was
advanced in twenty-six loans.

Bullion was exported :—

	Gold. ozs.		Silver. ozs.
1822	284,252		14,545,821
1823	296,373		11,568,258
1824	1,134,343		8,585,731
1825	1,273,323		5,566,399
	2,988,291		40,266,209

Gold . @ £3, 17s. 9d. = £11,616,981, 5s. 3d.
Silver . . . @ 5s. = £10,066,552, 5s. 0d.

Merchandise, too, of every description was
sent out in vast quantities. Every project that

could enter into the mind of man became an object of joint-stock enterprise, and every description of person in the realm, who could find the wherewithal, joined in one enterprise or another.

It has been computed by Mr. H. M. Hyndman that the loans to foreign States amounted to £86,000,000, and that in addition the following joint-stock companies were subscribed :—

20 Companies to build railways	£13,500,000
22 Bank and insurance companies	36,260,000
11 Gas companies	8,000,000
17 Foreign mining companies	18,200,000
8 English and Irish mining companies	10,580,000·
9 Companies for construction of canals, docks, and steamers	10,580,000
27 Companies for various industrial businesses	12,000,000
	£109,120,000

It is worthy of note that one of the projects of 1825 was the Manchester Ship Canal Company, with a capital of £1,000,000 in 10,000 shares of £100 each.

Under these influences there was a rise in prices, which was accentuated by other and even more pernicious directing powers. "It became" (says Mr. Tooke) "the business of speculators and

brokers to look minutely through the general
prices current, with a view to discover any
article that had not advanced, in order to
make it the subject of anticipated demand.   If
a person, not under the influence of the pre-
vailing delusion, inquired for what *reason* any
particular article had risen, the common answer
was, ' Everything else has risen, and therefore *this
ought to rise.*' "

The following is a picture of the mania that
had seized the whole community :—" Persons removed from all business, retired officers, widows
and single women of small fortune, risked their
incomes or their savings in every species of desper-
ate enterprise ; and the competition and scramble
for premiums in concerns which ought never to
have been otherwise than at a discount, were
perfectly astonishing to those who took no part
in these transactions."

By July 1825 the exchanges became unfavour-
able, and the Bank of England by private sales of
Exchequer Bills began to draw in its circulation.
Vast quantities of produce had been imported,
and, with the general lock-up of capital in the
various projects, there were no bills to pay for the
importations.   Hence gold had to be exported,
and as the demand became greater the Bank
became stiff about discounting, and further drew
in its issues.   The bill discounters followed suit,

and the London bankers refused accommodation
to their country correspondents. They in their
turn declined discounts offered by their clients,
and by December the whole of "Great Britain
and Ireland was in one scene of confusion, dismay,
and bankruptcy." The gold in the Bank of England had dwindled down until there was only
£1,261,000. The first great stoppage of banks
was that of Godfrey, Wentworth, & Co., of
London, with their branches at Bradford, Wakefield, and York. On 5th December Sir Peter
Pole & Co., after a struggle for a week, became
bankrupt. They were agents for about forty
country banks. Then followed during the next
six weeks crash after crash, mercantile and banking, of the latter alone about seventy.[1]

There were frequent Cabinet meetings, and the

---

[1] A moving account of the miseries of this period is given in
Harriet Martineau's "History of England during the Thirty Years'
Peace," book ii. chap. viii. :—

"There are some now of the most comfortable middle-class order
who cannot think of that year without bitter pain. They saw many
parents grow white-haired in a week's time : lovers parted on the eve
of marriage : light-hearted girls sent forth from the shelter of home
to learn to endure the destiny of the governess or the sempstress :
governesses, too old for a new station, going actually into the work-
house : rural gentry quitting their lands ; and whole families relin-
quishing every prospect in life and standing as bare as Lear and his
strange comrades on the heath. They saw something even worse than
all this. They saw the ties of family honour snapped by the strain of
cupidity first, and discontent afterwards, and the members falling off
from one another as enemies. They saw the hope of the innocent, the
faith of the pious, the charity of the generous, the integrity of the
trusted, giving way."

Mint worked day and night to turn out gold, which disappeared as fast as it was issued. The small notes of the Bank, £1 and £2, were reissued in the country, and were of help to allay the panic. Parliament reassembled on 2nd February 1826, and the question of the banking of the country was uppermost in every man's mind.

First and foremost the question of the small notes was finally settled. Power had been given, as noted above, to issue till 1833. It was seen that stringent measures were necessary, so on 22nd March 1826 an enactment forbade the further stamping on any notes under £5, and the date of the final abolition of all existing small notes was fixed at 5th April 1829.

Negotiations between the Government and the Bank of England resulted in the establishment of branches of the Bank in several provincial towns, and the granting of the privilege to form banks consisting of more than six partners. This was enacted by 7 Geo. IV. cap. 46, "An Act for the better regulating co-partnership of certain bankers in England." But the powerful and malign influence of the Bank of England prevented the latter provision from operation except at a distance of sixty-five miles from London. It was not till August 1833 that the evilly selfish policy of the Bank was compulsorily changed, and the benefit of joint-stock banking extended to the whole of England. Even now it is a blot on the Free Trade policy of England that the issue of notes by bankers, other than the Bank of England, should be prohibited in the circle of sixty-five miles radius around London.

But distress was universal, and although Government felt that this commercial crisis should work out its own salvation, it was constrained by force of circumstances to compel the unwilling Bank of England to make advances against produce. The amount was limited to three millions.

In Liverpool the Commissioners appointed by the Bank of England to administer the loan, in sums of not less than £500 nor more than £10,000, were John Ashton Case, Thomas Fletcher, David Hodgson, and Lister Ellis, with James Bunnell as Secretary. The committee rooms were over the Government office at the top of Water Street. The measures adopted proved successful, credit was gradually re-established, and the hoarded gold was again brought into circulation.

The establishment of branches of the Bank of England, and the formation of joint-stock banks, were not new ideas, but had, since the crises of 1819 and 1821, been discussed both publicly and privately, and the present crisis served as an opportunity for bringing them into being.[1]

For example, in Liverpool in 1822 the papers of the day stated that it was the intention of Government to permit the formation of joint-stock banks at a distance of not less than sixty-five miles from London, and that the principal merchants had had one or two private meetings. At the meetings the advantages of the Joint-Stock system were tabulated. The reasons given will now be read with interest :—

1. Capital, adequate for every contingency.
2. Safe deposit for capital.
3. An office for discount of respectable bills, free from the dangerous temptations, presented on the one hand by too great liberality, and the fatal consequences resulting, on the other, from a capricious reserve, in mercantile accommodation.
4. The means of allowing, on shortest notice,

[1] In November 1807 the Court of King's Bench granted a rule with a view of making inquiry into the legality of the formation of joint-stock companies. In 1822 Mr. Joplin, of Newcastle, issued a pamphlet in which he advocated the deleting of the clause in the Bank of England's charter which restricted banking co-partnerships of more than six persons. He communicated with several mercantile communities with reference to the matter, and in Liverpool some of the leading merchants memorialised the Ministers. Joplin originated the National Provincial Bank of England, and founded the *Economist*.

the most ample allowances on real securities; or on a regulated system of personal guarantee.

5. A secure basis for the issue (if it should be
thought desirable) of local notes, upon
such principles as will render them ex-
empt from the inconvenience and hazard
of private bankers' notes.

Also in 1817 we find rumours current in
Liverpool as to the establishment of branches
of the Bank of England in various parts of the
country.

The Bank of England opened branches at
Gloucester, Manchester, and Swansea, in the
order named, in 1826; followed in 1827 by
Birmingham, Liverpool, Bristol, and Leeds, in
1828 by Newcastle, in 1829 by Hull and
Norwich, and in 1834 by Plymouth and Ports-
mouth. A branch was opened at Exeter in
1827, but the business was removed to Plymouth in 1834.

This extended system of business was received
with a considerable amount of opposition. On
the one hand the already established banks
determined to compete for discounts. In 1827,
while the Bank of England was discounting
at 4 per cent., the Liverpool private banks were
quoting 3½ per cent., and the Manchester bankers

came to a resolution to discount at 3 per cent.
On the other hand, the Bank of England was
strenuously antagonistic to the scheme, but, like
Mercy, it has been found " to bless him that
gives and him that takes."

In objecting to the Bank of England poaching
on their preserves the country bankers had a real
grievance.   The Bank of England, in addition
to its other great privileges, had the right of
compounding for its stamp duties, while other
bankers had not.

It came to this, that the stamp duty on a bill
on London at 21 days' date cost the Bank of
England only 5d., whilst the cost to the country
banker was 3s. 6d., and that the cost of a circulation of £10,000 a year in £20 bills of exchange
was only £35 to the Bank of England, whilst it
cost the country banker £650.   This disparity
was too glaring to be passed over, and the Act 9
George IV. cap. 23 placed the country banks on
the same footing as the Bank of England as to
composition for stamp duties, and allowed them
to include in their composition bills up to 21
days' date.

The Bank of England also was opposed to the
granting of charters for the establishment of
joint-stock banks, and had hitherto been successful in prohibiting the issuing of drafts on London
for less than £50, but in 1829 the righteous

claims in these respects of the general banking community were ceded.

The first joint - stock bank to commence business in Liverpool was the Manchester and Liverpool District Bank, which took premises at 45 Pool Lane (now South Castle Street) in November 1829, under the management of James Baird. The date of the general commencement of the bank is given in the Report of the Select Committee of the House of Commons as 1st December 1829. On 16th May 1831 the Bank of Liverpool, the first joint-stock bank having its head office in Liverpool, was opened at 34 Brunswick Street, under the management of Joseph Langton.

The spread of the joint-stock system was gradual but general. In many cases the existing private bank was transformed into a joint-stock bank. But some of the wealthiest and most firmly founded private banks had an astonishing vitality, steadily resisting the popular wave.

Of the seven private banks of Liverpool existing in 1830, two became in the next few years joint-stock banks, one failed, and another did not become a joint-stock bank till late in the forties—Barned's Bank. Of the remaining three, Moss & Co. was converted in the year 1864 into the North-Western Bank, and the latter amalgamated with the London City and

Midland Bank Ltd. in 1897; A. Heywood,
Sons, & Co. was sold to the Bank of Liverpool
in 1883; whilst Leyland & Bullins endured till
1901, when it amalgamated with the North and
South Wales Bank Ltd.

CHAPTER III

BANKERS AND BANKING.

Origin of private bankers—Issue of country notes—Dining hour in
Liverpool—Bank holidays—Currency of bills—Coinage and
currency—Bank of England notes—Depreciation of bank notes—
Fictitious payees—Bankers' commission—Generosity of Liverpool bankers—Early nineteenth-century Christian names—Dress
of bankers of eighteenth and early nineteenth centuries.

BEFORE proceeding to a detailed account of the
several banking houses of Liverpool, it will be
well to consider who were bankers, and what
were the conditions of banking.

The banker of this early period was a merchant,
or larger trader, who grafted the business of banking on to his own affairs. He would have an
account with some London banker for the purpose
of paying his acceptances for the produce in which
he dealt, and for the collection or discounting
of the acceptances he received. Some of his
neighbours, whose businesses were not so extensive, found it a convenience to pass their
transactions through the more substantial man,
and it was a convenience to the London banker
also, as it avoided the multiplicity of small

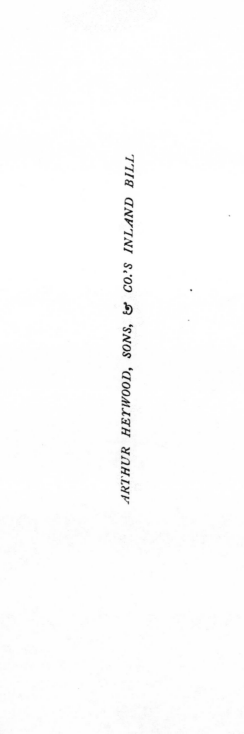

ARTHUR HETWOOD, SONS, & CO.'S INLAND BILL

No. _____

£ _____

Liverpool Bank

Mess.rs Joseph Denison & Co

London

Ent.d Per

accounts. Then the savings of the people were intrusted to the merchant, whose probity and success had begotten confidence. So the business grew, and gradually came the development from trader and banker to banker pure and simple.

The business of discounting acceptances and promissory notes, the collection of bills and country notes, the remittance of payments, and the retirement of acceptances now formed his daily business. For the purpose of remittance the banker would either issue his own notes, or his draft on his London "correspondent," as the London agent was then called. For the purpose of implementing the London account he would send up notes of various bankers, acceptances, and occasionally specie. In Liverpool bankers did not issue notes, but drafts only, " at one or two months' date, as has been the usual and customary practice." And, indeed, Lancashire generally was averse from the system of local notes. Far otherwise was it in the neighbouring Yorkshire and most other parts of the kingdom. In time of trouble the use of local notes led to much disaster. After the passing of the Bank Restriction Act the number of issuing bankers rapidly increased, and the notes varied in value from *eighteenpence* in Yorkshire and the Isle of Wight to the usual guinea and £5 notes.

In 1807, *apropos* of the failure of many banks in Yorkshire, Billinge in his *Liverpool Advertiser* thus delivers himself :—

"We have ever been of opinion (and our opinion is justified by daily experience) that the circulation of provincial bankers' paper is highly injurious to the public interests, because it enables speculative, designing, and often *pennyless* men to create a false capital, and thereby to enter into schemes which too frequently involve thousands in ruin ; for, having nothing to lose themselves, they run, *neck or nothing*, into the wildest and most extravagant adventures, careless of the consequences. To the honour of Lancashire be it known, not a single note is issued by any banking house in the county ; and notwithstanding the magnitude of its manufactures, commerce, and population, nothing is current but Bank of England paper and sterling specie : nor is the least inconvenience experienced in consequence of this wise regulation."

The bulk of the Liverpool bankers arose out of general merchants, some few from tea-dealers, and one from linen merchants. In the majority of cases, after declaring themselves bankers, their trading business was conducted hand-in-hand with the banking business; that is to say, though mainly bankers, they had subsidiary businesses. But the more successful bankers gradually freed themselves from such entanglements, and relied entirely on banking.

As with the general merchant, so the banker

resided over his business premises. In the case
of several partners, the junior generally occupied
the bank house. The hours of attendance were
at first from 9 to 1 and 3 to 6. The interval
was the regular dining "hour" of the community. With reference to this Dr. Currie
writes in 1792 :—

"Sixty years ago people returned from Exchange
about 12.30, and generally sat down to Dinner before
than after one. In 1780 the general Hour was
2 o'clock—half-an-Hour after on set Days, or sometimes 3 with the Highest Quality. When the late
Mr. Kennion became Collector of the Customs,[1] that
he might enjoy himself the more, the Custom House
Hours underwent an alteration, and instead of 2 Hours
allowed from 12 to 2, the usual time allowed for
Dinner, the House was kept open and Business
transacted until 3 o'clock—when publick Business
closed for the day. This brought the new Hours
of regulation in Business, and those who had Business
to transact now seldom sit down until after 3 o'clock
—the general dining Hour is now got from 3 to 5,
some people go later."

From the minute-book of "The Unanimous
Society"—a Liverpool club who dined regularly
together—we find that in 1769 the hour was 2,
2.30 in 1775, and 3 in 1777.

Agreeably to this we find the bankers con-

[1] In 1782.

forming to the new state of things, and in June
1784 they issued the following circular :—

"Messrs. Wm. Clarke & Sons, Arthur Heywood,
Son, & Co., and Charles Caldwell & Co. acquaint their
friends and the public that after the 12th inst. the hours
for transacting public business at their respective banks
will be from nine to three o'clock, and on Thursdays
from nine to one as usual."

The reason for the shorter hours on Thursday
was that that was the blank post-day to London,
and hence the business community took its half-
holiday on that day. By 1790 the mail service
to London had been so accelerated that Friday
had become the short day.

With reference to the closing of the banks
between one and three, it is well to recall
the fact that the employees probably all lived
within easy distance of their work. The
population was small; in 1760 it was only
25,787, and by 1801 it had increased to only
77,708.

Bank holidays as such were not, but the
number of public holidays was large. In process
of time these, through the influence of the
Gradgrinds of commerce, became beautifully less,
until "St. Lubbock smiled, and all the world was
gay." As a matter of interest, a list of the public
holidays in 1811, extracted from Maberly Phillips'

" History of Banks in the North of England," is
subjoined :—

Jan. 1.	New Year's Day.	May 29.	Restoration of
„ 18.	Queen's Birthday.		Charles II.
„ 30.	King Charles'	June 3.	Whit Monday.
	Martyrdom.	„ 4.	Whit Tuesday.
Feb. 27.	Ash Wednesday.	Oct. 25.	King's Accession.
Apr. 12.	Good Friday.	Nov. 5.	Gunpowder Plot.
„ 15.	Easter Monday.	Dec. 25.	Christmas Day.
„ 16.	Easter Tuesday.	„ 26.	St. Stephen's Day.
May 23.	Holy Thursday.	„ 27.	St. John's Day.

With the necessary alteration of date in the
case of the " Movable Feasts," this list will stand
good for the period we are considering, say, 1760
to 1820.

The currency of bills varied greatly. Reference
has been made earlier to the bankers' inland drafts
at one or two months' date. Owing to the uncertain length of the sailing-ship voyages, and
the perils of privateers and pirates, the time
required for the realisation of the produce varied
greatly. Hence credit was elastic. Bills at the
following terms were known at this period: 90
days' sight, 3, 6, 9, 12, 13, 14, 16, 18, 24, 30, 36,
and 42 months' date. For the ordinary course
of business these would be drawn against produce.
Hence it is not so surprising, as it would seem
at first blush, that during the parlous times of

1809–16 frequent sales by public auction are made of bills, of which the drawer or the acceptor or the endorser was insolvent. Sometimes both drawer and acceptor, and occasionally drawer, acceptor, and endorser, were all insolvent. Yet being based on produce there was a certain value attaching to this paper, and a shrewd speculator, possessed of some ready money, might well make a good profit out of the necessities of the situation. The practice of drawing bills for sums including halfpence was current. An item in the parish accounts for 1794 reads, " Estate of C. Caldwell & Co., returned bills £879, 15s. 5½d."

From 1793 to the resumption of cash payments in 1825–6 the currency of the country was in an unsatisfactory condition. Large amounts of coin had from time to time been issued by the Mint, but the foreign drain for payment to troops, for subsidies to allies, and for the purchase of corn, owing to the failure of harvest, rapidly denuded the country of all full-weight gold. The coins in use were the guinea, half, third, and quarter guinea, with silver crown, half-crown, shilling, and sixpence. Copper halfpence had been in use from about 1670–80, but the copper penny first saw light in 1797, the weight being one ounce. That huge cart-wheel of a coin, the copper twopence, weighing two ounces, was put into circulation in that year,

and in that year only. On 1st July 1817 the
sovereign and half-sovereign were brought out,
entirely supplanting all other gold coins.

In aid of the currency the Bank of England in
1804 issued a large number of Spanish dollars,
then in their possession, with a small head of
George the Third overstamped on that of Ferdi-
nand of Spain ; whereupon a bitter wit of the
period wrote :

> " The Bank to make its Spanish dollars pass
> Stamped the head of a fool on the head of an ass."

They were issued at 5s. 6d. each, and were in
circulation for many years. The Bank fixed the
date of their redemption at 1st November 1816,
but extended this to February and again to May
1817. After this they agreed to accept all others
tendered at 5s. each. The Bank also issued silver
tokens of 3s. and 1s. 6d. each.

Prior to 1759 no Bank of England notes were
issued under £20. In that year £10 notes were
issued, and were followed in 1793 by £5 notes.
In 1797, when the Bank Restriction Act was
passed, enabling the Bank of England to dispense
with its obligation to pay coin for its notes on
demand, the addition of £1 and £2 notes was
made to the currency.

The inflated issue of non-convertible notes produced in the first place a large amount of hoard-

ing of gold coin. In many cases it was found,
when wealthy men died, that they had large
stores of hoarded guineas. The next result was
an appreciation of gold and a depreciation of the
paper currency. A Bullion Committee sat in
1810 to consider the question, and in May 1811
Parliament fatuously passed a resolution declaring
a £1 note and one shilling equal to one guinea,
whereas it was notorious that in the outside
market the value of the guinea was 25s. It is
well to record here the discount on Bank of
England notes during this period :—

In 1802	from 7½ to 8⅓ discount.
From 1803–9	£2 13 2 ,,
1810	13 9 6 ,,
1812	20 15 0 ,,
1813	23 0 0 ,,
1814	25 0 0 ,,

Through the bankruptcies of 1815 and 1816,
brought on by the heavy reduction of inflated
prices, caused by the pernicious system of currency, the Bank of England note was raised in
value until in October 1816 the discount was
only £1, 8s. 6d. per cent. But this was attained
at the sole expense of the public.

Banking law was naturally in a very immature
stage. Many and costly have been the decisions,
and innumerable the enactments, by which the

law, broadening "slowly down from precedent to precedent," has established banking usages. An account of these is not within the scope of this book. But an instance or two arising out of early transactions will not be out of place. In 1788 Livesey, Hargreave, Anstie, Smith, & Hill failed. They were merchants in the Manchester business in a very large way, so large, in fact, that public meetings of merchants took place in Manchester and Liverpool for the purpose of maintaining the credit of certain of their paper, lest public credit might unduly suffer. Although men of large estates, they had traded beyond their means, and to supplement the latter had established "drawing posts," and thereby had put a deal of fictitious paper into circulation. One of the points that had to be decided was the status of these bills drawn in favour of fictitious payees and negotiated through third persons.

Further the Usury Acts were in force, and the same bankruptcy gave rise to the question whether the bankers' charge of $\frac{1}{4}$ per cent. commission for discounting bills, in addition to the current rate of interest, did not bring the charge under the Usury Acts. This was decided by Lord Kenyon and a jury in the negative.

From the detailed accounts of the various bankers it will be seen that a considerable proportion of them interested themselves in the affairs

of the town. The rise of the joint-stock banks
withdrew this class of man from the public service. On the Reformed Town Council of 1835
only one banker, Samuel Hope, was elected.

During the recurring public distresses which
arose during the Napoleonic wars the old bankers
were regularly generous. They recognised their
public position, and gave accordingly ; to the charities of the town they were liberal, and took prominent part in the government of their activities.

The various news-rooms had their strong
support, as had also the New Exchange buildings.
The Liverpool Gas Company had for some years
bankers as its directors. But in one case they
failed, and failed unanimously, to look broadly
into the future. When, in 1827, a motion was
brought forward to enable the Town Council to
erect a public building on the site of the Old
Infirmary Gardens, in the minority of seven were
found all the bankers, Henry Moss, Samuel
Thompson, and Richard Leyland. Had their
views prevailed, we should have had no St.
George's Hall.

It is noticeable that from the latter part of the
eighteenth and the commencement of the nineteenth century begins locally the custom of using
surnames, generally the maiden name of the
mother, as part of the fore-names given to the
offspring. Before this time the ordinary simple

LIVERPOOL EXCHANGE, 1820

"Christian" names were used. Taking only those who have been, or are, connected with banking, we find numerous examples.

John Gladstone on 29th April 1800 married Miss Robertson. One of his sons was Robertson Gladstone.

Samuel Sandbach on 15th September 1802 married Miss Eliza Robertson, daughter of Rev. Dr. Robertson of Kiltcarn. To-day we have Gilbert Robertson Sandbach.

On 24th March 1806 Hugh Jones married Elizabeth Heywood. There exists a large family of Heywood Joneses.

On 9th October 1806 James Wood married Miss Marke; hence J. Marke Wood.

On 1st September 1820 George Holt married Emma Durning. One of Liverpool's latest honorary freemen is Robert Durning Holt.

The dress of the banker of the period, which was equally that of the merchant and others of the upper and middle classes, was vastly different from the dress of to-day. Brooke ("Ancient Liverpool," p. 257) gives a full account of this:—

"They then commonly wore coats cut much in the form of court dress-coats, often with stand-up collars, and usually with gilt, silvered, twisted, or basket buttons; waistcoats of very great length, of the kind called flap waistcoats, the flaps being large, and containing pockets with a small cover or flap over each pocket, and often with ornamented basket buttons; short breeches, with buckles of gold, silver, or false stones, at the knees, and large buckles of gold or silver, or gilt or plated to resemble those metals, in their shoes. The coat, waistcoat, and breeches were often all of one colour, frequently of a light or snuff colour. Ruffles at the wrist, and white stocks for the throat were almost invariably worn. Cocked hats were commonly used; the kind of cocked hat then in fashion came to a point or peak in front, and the raised part of the back was higher than the sides. . . . The young men, and some of the middle-aged men, wore their hair dressed with curls on each side of the face, called cannon curls, and with queues behind, and occasionally thick short queues called clubs. Wigs of various descriptions, such as tie wigs, cauliflower wigs, brown bob wigs, and bush wigs, with hair powder, were also commonly worn by middle-aged and elderly persons. . . . The stockings worn by them were generally of silk, sometimes plain, and at other times ribbed or striped, and in the morning occasionally of cotton or woollen yarns.

Canes and walking-sticks were very generally used, with large heads of gold, and sometimes of silver, amber, and ebony.

Boots were rarely used, except the kind called topboots, which were commonly worn by equestrians.

CHAPTER IV

JOHN WYKE.

Vixerunt fortes ante "Arthur Heywooda."

John Wyke—Watch-tool industry—Wyke's Court—Academy of Paint-
ing and Sculpture—Dispensary—"The Octagonians."

OF the doubtless numerous merchants who performed the office of bankers to the rising commercial community of Liverpool there is little
record left. There were in the early days no
newspaper and no directory. Hence since they
lacked those who could preserve their fame, their
names have perished. But by good chance one
name has been preserved, and this by the accident
of his public notice announcing his withdrawal
from the banking business. "Mr. John Wyke of
Liverpool having declined the banking business,
all persons having any bills drawn on him are
desired to apply to John Menzies in Williamson
Square, who is appointed to settle the same, and
all persons indebted to the said John Wyke for
bills drawn by him, or on notes, bonds, &c., are
desired immediately to pay the same to the said

John Menzies. 17th September 1773." This is
the sole record we possess of a banker anterior
to the establishment of those firms whose names
are recorded in the directories.

In their several histories, Brooke, Stonehouse,
and Picton all speak well of John Wyke, but
the author is grateful that they have left to
him the pleasure of making this addition to
our knowledge of him.

Now what manner of man was John Wyke
that pleasure should be found in this discovery?
Picton shall answer: "A man probably little
known beyond his immediate sphere, but who
within that sphere fulfilled all the duties of a
good citizen, and exercised a beneficial influence
in his day and generation."

Born in Prescot, a few miles from Liverpool,
in 1720, he was brought up in the great industry
of the place, the manufacture of watch tools and
movements. He acquired celebrity in his business, and in 1758 opened premises in King Street,
Liverpool, being the first to introduce watchmaking to that town. He had before leaving
Prescot bought land, and had a house in Dale
Street, Liverpool, immediately opposite the end
of Crosshall Street, and in 1764–5 the property
was rebuilt. Here he constructed Wyke's Court,
which was laid out for his residence, coach-house,
stables, garden, manufactory, warehouse, and

WYKE'S COURT, DALE STREET, THE RESIDENCE OF JOHN WYKE, 1765

various other buildings, all disposed about a large
rectangular courtyard. The house lay to the
north, next the garden, which stretched towards
Tithebarn Street. The entrance to the whole
was on the south-west side, under an archway
from Dale Street. Here John Wyke conducted
his business as a watch and clock and watch-tool
manufacturer. Here also would be conducted
his banking business.

When the Royal Academy was established in
1768 some of the Liverpool artists and amateurs
met together, and in the following year formed
a society upon similar lines. Among these appears the name of John Wyke. The society was
not very successful, but it paved the way for the
various exhibitions which have fostered the art
feeling in Liverpool, and which have their cul-
mination in the Walker Art Gallery. The
rooms taken by the society were in [North]
John Street, in a house which was then the home
of the Liverpool Library, now located at the
Lyceum, Bold Street.

In 1778 John Wyke was prominent amongst
the gentlemen who established the first dispensary in Liverpool. This was also in [North] John
Street, at the northern corner of Princes Street,
the site of the new buildings of the Royal Insurance Company. In the report of the first year
of the dispensary John Wyke's name appears as

auditor, and for many years he took an active interest in the affairs of this valuable charity. It is stated by Stonehouse ("Streets of Liverpool") that the origin of the dispensary was due to John Wyke.[1]

That magnificent charity, the Blue Coat School, also found a friend in him, and in his will, while remembering his native town of Prescot, he benefited the Blue Coat Hospital, the Infirmary and Dispensary of Liverpool.

The watchmaking business was conducted by John Wyke alone until about 1774, when he took Thomas Green (probably his brother-in-law) into partnership. This continued till his death, 10th September 1787, he being then sixty-seven years of age. He was buried at Prescot. The funeral procession from Liverpool was preceded as far as the foot of Low Hill by the boys of the Blue Coat School singing a funeral anthem, and on its entrance into Prescot the children of the school there met, and preceded it to the church, singing on the way. He was buried in an altar tomb he had erected to the memory of his parents, whose ancestors had resided in that parish for nearly three centuries,

[1] In 1782 the dispensary was removed to a specially erected building in Church Street, adjoining the Athenæum. The number of persons benefited from 1778 to 1809 was 362,541, being at the average of about 12,000 a year. In 1829 the establishment was removed to the new dispensary in Vauxhall Road, called the North Dispensary.

and his epitaph was written by his friend William
Roscoe.

He had married twice. His first wife, Ann, is
advertised thus on 7th August 1760: "Whereas
Ann, my wife, eloped from me on 27th day of
April last without my knowledge," &c. On
18th August 1768 John Wyke married his
second wife, Miss Jane Green. The entry in
the *Liverpool Chronicle* is noteworthy: "Mr.
Wyke, famous for instruments in the watch
way, to Miss Green." She was appointed
executrix under his will, dated 9th April 1783,
which was drawn up by William Roscoe. Pre-
sumably she was considerably younger than her
late husband, for, continuing her residence in
Wyke's Court till 1790, she on 29th July of
that year married Joseph Jewett of Kingston-
upon-Hull.

His partner, Thomas Green, continued the
business till at least 1811. By 1796, however,
some of the buildings within the court were
converted into tenement houses, and quite a little
colony of watchmaking artisans were collected
there.

In the sixth volume of the "Proceedings of the
Historic Society of Lancashire and Cheshire" there
is an etching of John Wyke's house as it appeared
in 1819. This was immediately anterior to the
acquisition of the premises by the Gas Company,

who here erected gasworks. The site of John Wyke's property is now covered by the Central Police Offices, the Stipendiary Magistrate's Court, and the Fire Brigade Central Offices.

About 1763 certain seceders from the dissenting (or practically Unitarian) congregations of Key Street and Benn's Gardens built a chapel in the open district between Dale Street and Whitechapel, which, when built on later, became known as The Temple. This chapel was called "The Octagon," from the shape of the building, which had been designed by a watchmaker named Joseph Finney. John Wyke, originally of the faith of the Church of England, was induced by his friend Bentley, well known later on as the friend and partner of Josiah Wedgwood, to join this congregation. The reason for the secession was that the members desired a liturgical service. But the chapel did not continue long in the new faith, as the final sermon was preached in 1776, and the building, of which the interior effect is described as "light, cheerful, and agreeable," was bought by a minister of the Church of England, and under the title of St. Catherine's Church was administered in that faith until 1820, when it was taken down. Wyke on the break-up of the congregation in 1776 reverted to his old faith.

On 8th January 1852 a paper on the "Dis-

continued Churches of Liverpool" was read
before the Historic Society of Lancashire and
Cheshire, and the book of liturgy used by the
Octagon congregation, which was then shown in
illustration, bore on its title-page the name of
John Wyke.

CHAPTER V

WILLIAM CLARKE AND SONS.

Wm. Clarke & Sons—Transition from linen draper to merchant, then
to banker—Partners—Liverpool Literary Coterie—Inquiry into
finances of the firm—Accession of Wm. Roscoe—Particulars of his
life—Chat Moss—Lorenzo de Medici—Joined by Thos. Leyland
—Election of Wm. Roscoe as M.P. for Liverpool—Secession of
Thomas Leyland—Subsidiary businesses—Suspension of the firm—
Bankruptcy—Sale of books, pictures, &c., of Wm. Roscoe and
John Clarke—Sales of landed property—Death of Wm. Roscoe
—Roscoe, Clarke, Wardell & Co.—Lowry, Roscoe & Wardell—
Fletcher, Roberts, Roscoe & Co.—Account of Thomas Fletcher—
Bankruptcy of Fletcher, Roberts, Roscoe & Co.—Annulment of
the bankruptcy of Roscoe, Clarke & Roscoe.

THE origin of this bank was in the linen trade.
At the date of the earliest Liverpool directory,
1766, William Clarke was a linen draper, residing
over his business premises on the east side of Derby
Square. It was at the junction of Castle Street
and the north side of Harrington Street. In
1769 he is described as "merchant and linen
draper," and by 1774 he appears as "banker and
linen draper," and has thus the honour of being
the first banker of Liverpool recorded as such in
the local directory. The transition from tradesman to merchant, and then the further progres-

sion to banker, is typical of the bankers of this
period. In the directory of 1777 appeared for
the first time " William Clarke & Sons, Bankers,"
the linen business being still in the name of
William Clarke alone. The sons were William,
then aged 24, and John, aged 21. In July 1781
Mrs. Clarke died, and the idea of discontinuing
the linen business then seemed to arise. The
parting of the ways was shown by the advertisement of 20th September 1781 of the sale
of the entire stock of William Clarke's linen,
drapery, and millinery articles. Thenceforward
the Clarkes were bankers, the business being conducted in Harrington Street, just round the
corner from the old linen warehouse. William
Clarke about this time purchased a considerable
quantity of land in Everton, then an unspoiled
suburb, and built before 1790 a large mansion
for himself. He also built a villa on Hillside,
Everton, for his mother, and a further house for
his son William on the east side of Everton
Terrace. He also, on 9th October 1783, took
unto himself a second wife, Mrs. Ellen Shaw.
The other son, John Clarke, by 1790 was living
at Birchfield, Folly Lane (now Islington). A
year or two earlier he had joined on to his partnership in the bank a coal business, the offices
of which were at Canal Basin. He, in conjunction with William Roscoe, Charles Porter, and

Wm. German, had acquired and opened out in 1789 a colliery at Orrell. Clarke dealt exclusively in Orrell and cannel coal. At this period William Roscoe lived in Folly Lane, in a house a little south of Mansfield Street. He and William Clarke, junior, were intimate friends, and formed the leaders of the small band of young men who studied classic authors in the early morning hours before business. They too, with Dr. Currie and Dr. Shepherd, formed "The Liverpool Literary Coterie," whose hospitality, as an unlicked cub of sixteen, De Quincey enjoyed, and on whose memory he, after years of debauchery had dulled his moral feelings, scattered the venom of ingratitude. When he wrote, three of the four whom he maligned were dead. *Ingratum si dixeris, omnia dixisti.*

William Clarke, junior, was delicate, and had to pass the winter of 1789 in Italy. He chose Florence as his place of abode, and as at this time Roscoe had resolved on writing the life of Lorenzo de Medici, the occasion was seized for searching in the Laurentian and Ricardi libraries for original and interesting matter. The result was beyond all expectation, and among other valuable discoveries were the poems of Lorenzo, which had escaped the notice of all previous biographers.

On 2nd July 1790 William Clarke lost his second wife. The firm continued to progress,

CLARKES & *ROSCOE'S* *BANK,* 1792
Corner of Dale Street and Castle Street

and although doubtless distressed by the panic
of 1793, they suffered no serious misfortune.
They by 1792 had acquired more central premises
at the corner of Castle Street and Dale Street, the
front door of the bank facing the Town Hall.
William Clarke, junior, then took up his residence in the bank house.

On 5th February 1797 William Clarke died,
aged 73, and the business was continued by the
two sons.

On 16th June in the following year William
Clarke, junior, married, at Kendal, Miss Ann
Pedder of that town, and in April 1799 he was
blessed with a son.

In looking into matters, after the death of
William Clarke, the business of the house was
found to be involved. The London correspondents were Esdaile & Co., and Sir Benjamin
Hammett, one of the partners of that firm,
came down to Liverpool to investigate. Esdailes
held about £200,000 of Clarke & Sons' paper.
William Roscoe was called in in his professional
capacity as attorney, and Sir Benjamin Hammett
was so struck by the ability he displayed in
arranging the affairs of the firm that he proposed
that he should become a partner with the Clarkes.
Roscoe repeatedly refused, and was only won
over to consent upon Hammett threatening to
put the matter into bankruptcy. Roscoe had,

by his examination of the affairs, satisfied himself that in ordinary times there were sufficient assets to cover all liabilities. Thus the great William Roscoe entered the noble army of bankers.

It is needless here to enter otherwise than briefly into the particulars of Roscoe's early life, as fuller information is readily accessible.

Born on the 8th March 1753, the only son of William and Elizabeth Roscoe, at the "Old Bowling-Green House," Martindale's Hill (now Mount Pleasant), then kept by his parents, William Roscoe had few advantages in early life. He left school at the early age of 12, and at 16, after a short sojourn in John Gore's bookseller's shop, was apprenticed to Mr. John Eyes, an attorney. At the conclusion of his articles he entered into partnership with Samuel Aspinall (or Aspinwall), and continued in this profession, first with that gentleman, and afterwards with him and Joshua Lace, until September 1792, when the partnership terminated. In 1796 he retired on a well-earned competency. He married on 22nd February 1781 Jane, the second daughter of William Griffies, linen draper, of Castle Street, Liverpool. He resided successively in School Lane, Rainford Gardens, Toxteth Park, near the Dingle, until in 1793 he removed to Birchfield, Islington, where he had bought

WILLIAM ROSCOE

some land and erected a house. In 1792 he associated himself with Thomas Wakefield, a sugar refiner of Liverpool, in attempts to reclaim Chat Moss and Trafford Moss. The early experiments seemed to promise so well that they formed strong reasons for Roscoe resigning his legal profession. He hoped to turn his bent for agriculture and horticulture to profitable account, but it finally entailed on him a heavy lock-up of capital. His magnum opus, "The Life of Lorenzo de Medici," appeared in the winter of 1795. In 1799 he purchased half the estate of Allerton, including the Hall, from the representatives of Mrs. Hardman, and took up his abode there on 18th March of that year. The estate thus purchased was about 153 acres.

In the following year, as noted above, he was induced, through reasons of friendship, to forsake his retirement and enter into commercial life.

The style of the firm now became "Clarkes and Roscoe."

In 1802 a very considerable addition to the strength of the firm was made. They were joined by Thomas Leyland, a very wealthy merchant, and hard-headed, keen business man, and the firm now became "Leyland, Clarkes, and Roscoe." Full notice of Thomas Leyland will be found under "Leyland & Bullins."

William Clarke had always been of delicate

health, and on 21st October 1805 he died[1] in
his fifty-second year, at the house of Robert Holt
Leigh, Esq., M.P., Duke Street, Westminster.
A close personal friend of William Roscoe from
early youth, they were bound by ties not only of
affection, but of congenial literary tastes.   Clarke,
although of a retiring disposition, had genuine
talent and extensive learning.   The mansion that
William Clarke the elder had built at Everton,
and which latterly had been tenanted by his son,
now deceased, was sold early in 1806, and became
the property of Nicholas Waterhouse.

In November 1806 a parliamentary election
took place, and the friends of liberty, civil and
religious, nominated William Roscoe as one of
the candidates, and triumphantly placed him at
the head of the poll.   The defeated candidate,
General Banastre Tarleton, wrote to the press,
boldly stating, "The wealth of my opponents has
been the cause of my discomfiture, and corruption
the means of their success."

Under date 31st December 1806 appeared the
following circular:—

"The partnership heretofore carried on in Liverpool
by the undersigned Thomas Leyland, John Clarke, and
William Roscoe, all of that place, bankers, under the

---

[1] His wife survived him till 8th December 1831, when she died at
her residence, Castle End, Gloucester.

firm of Leyland, Clarke, & Roscoe, is this day, by
mutual consent, dissolved.

(Signed)   THOS. LEYLAND.
             JOHN CLARKE.
             WM. ROSCOE." [1]

The firm in 1807 appears as "Roscoe, Clarke,
and Roscoe," the latest accession being William
Stanley Roscoe, eldest son of William Roscoe.
He resided with his father at Allerton Hall.

In this year there was another parliamentary

[1] The reasons for this withdrawal by Thomas Leyland are not at all
clear. The Life of William Roscoe, by his son, simply mentions the
matter thus: "Unfortunately, soon after his election, his partner,
Thomas Leyland, whose name stood at the head of the firm, and
whose wealth contributed to its stability, withdrew suddenly from the
partnership."

Picton ("Memorials of Liverpool," vol. ii. p. 142, ed. 1875)
attributed it to Leyland foreseeing financial disaster to the firm.
This is doubtful. Picton seems to have taken the phrasing from a
character sketch by "An Old Stager," and to have hastily adduced it
as a clue to the present position. But it is quite probable that Leyland
dissociated himself from the firm on account of Roscoe's strong
support of the movement for the abolition of the slave trade, then
agitating the country, and which had a successful outcome in Parliament early in 1807. Leyland had for years been drawing thousands
and tens of thousands from the "African" trade, and as the love of
money was his dearest love, it is not improbable that the possible
drying-up of one of the great sources of his wealth had something
to do with the dissolution of the partnership. Further, keen and
sagacious though Thomas Leyland was, it would require a greater
foresight than even he had to gauge the storm and stress of the next
ten years, particularly years of crises like 1808-9-10-12 and 1815 and
1816.

It is also probable that Leyland preferred to fight for his own hand.
He had during his three years' connection with the Clarkes acquired a
knowledge of the mystery of banking, and possibly thought the time
had arrived for him to commence business on his own account.

election, and William Roscoe was again nominated, but retired before the election.

Like most of the bankers of their time, the Roscoes had subsidiary businesses. It has been already mentioned that John Clarke had a separate coal business, concerning himself entirely with Orrell and Wigan coal. The Roscoes also embarked in the same business, being importers of Bagillt coal, having their office at Nova Scotia, Liverpool. They also burdened themselves with interests in a colliery and smelting works at Bagillt, while William Roscoe continued to take considerable interest in the Chat Moss lands.

At the conclusion of the Napoleonic war in 1816 there was a commercial panic, owing to the great fall in prices which the peace produced. Their resources being locked up, Roscoe, Clarke, and Roscoe had the misfortune to be unable to meet their engagements, and notice to that effect appeared in the local press on 1st February 1816. On 3rd February there was a meeting of the creditors of the bank.[1]

The account of this meeting, given in Gore's *Liverpool Advertiser*, has a quaint flavour :—

---

[1] Picton ("Memorials," vol. ii. p. 22, ed. 1875) gives the date of the suspension as 1818, and he has been followed by some incautious writers. The bank by arrangement lingered on till 1820, when the three partners were formally made bankrupt.

"A meeting of the creditors of Messrs. Roscoe,
Clarke, & Roscoe was held at the Great Room of
Lillyman's Hotel on Saturday last, when a statement
of the concerns of the house was produced by Mr.
Roscoe, from which it appeared that the debts of the
bank did not exceed £315,000, for the liquidation of
which, the means that were shown, afforded not only
perfect satisfaction to the creditors, but a gratifying
assurance of a handsome surplus ultimately arising to
the partners of the house. Mr. Roscoe submitted the
statement with great feeling, but in a clear, energetic,
and manly tone. He was received, he was heard, and
he retired, accompanied with the strongest testimony of
attachment and respect ; and though he solicited inquiry
in a very pointed and earnest manner, a single question
was not put to him. When we consider the occasion,
nothing, assuredly, could be more gratifying or honour-
able to all the parties."

The state of affairs was investigated by a committee of seven, and a report was printed and
laid before the public. It was estimated that,
after the payment of all debts, there would be
an eventual surplus to the partners of £61,144.
But alas for such roseate views! After four
years' struggle to realise the assets, William
Roscoe and his partners had to become bankrupts.
The more easily realisable assets were at once put
on the market for sale. These comprised the
books, pictures, prints, &c., belonging to William
Roscoe, and some valuable pictures belonging to
John Clarke. Roscoe's library realised £5150,

his prints £1886, and the pictures £3239.
Among the last named were a portrait of Leo X.,
and a head of Christ by Leonardo da Vinci, both
of which were bought by the eminent agriculturist
Thomas Coke[1] of Holkham (whose hospitality
Roscoe had enjoyed in 1814), at a cost of £500
and 300 guineas respectively. The sale took place
on 29th July 1816 and thirteen following days.[2]

The several estates belonging to the partners
were also advertised for sale. These were:
Allerton Hall and 153 acres of land, belonging
to William Roscoe; Orrell House, with gardens,

[1] Created Earl of Leicester in 1837.

[2] One ventures to reproduce here William Roscoe's sonnet on parting from his library. It was handed about among his friends in
manuscript, and appeared in the *Liverpool Advertiser* 9th September
1816, and *Liverpool Mercury* 13th September 1816:—

> " As one who destined from his friends to part
>   Regrets his loss, yet hopes again erewhile
>   To share their converse and enjoy their smile,
>   And tempers, as he may, affliction's dart—
> Thus, loved associates! chiefs of elder art!
>   Teachers of wisdom! who could once beguile
>   My tedious hours, and lighten ev'ry toil,
>   I now resign you; nor with fainting heart—
> For pass a few short years, or days, or hours,
>   And happier seasons may their dawn unfold,
>   And all your sacred fellowship restore;
> When freed from earth, unlimited its powers,
>   Mind shall with mind direct communion hold,
>   And kindred spirits meet to part no more."

At the sale of books some of Roscoe's friends bought volumes to the
value of £600 and wished to present them to him, but he gratefully
declined. The books were then given to the Liverpool Athenæum,
where they now form a distinct portion of the library.

pinery, and conservatories, with about 52 acres
of land, belonging to John Clarke; Crook Hall,
near Wigan, and 49 acres of land, the property
of John Clarke; Skipton Pastures, about $16\frac{1}{2}$
acres, on the road from Bolton to Chorley;
Dumplington Farm, about 38 acres, 4 miles from
Manchester; Barton Park Farm, 400 acres, about
7 miles from Manchester; Barton Grange, and
about 200 acres of moss ground; sundry tracts of
Chat Moss, about 2000 acres; smelting works at
Bagillt.   There were interests in collieries at Orrell
and Bagillt; also a small estate belonging to John
Clarke, "The Springs," Orrell, and "The Crooke,"
Sherrington, an estate of 6 acres in Ashton.

John Clarke's pictures were removed from his
house, Orrell Mount, to be sold in Manchester,
9th and 10th January 1817.[1]

The landed estates did not sell readily; indeed,
many of them were still in hand when, on
18th January 1820, a commission in bankruptcy
was issued against William Roscoe, John Clarke,
and William Stanley Roscoe.

[1] In the "Autobiography of Thomas Fletcher" (privately printed),
Fletcher records how in 1821 he bought Hilton's picture of "Lear
and his Daughters," at Winstanley's Rooms, Liverpool, at the sale of
John Clarke's pictures, for 31 guineas, it having cost Clarke 120 guineas.
Hence all Clarke's pictures could not have been sold at the earlier
date. Little did Fletcher then imagine that he, then senior partner
in Fletcher, Yates & Co., would in after years be a partner in the
firm that tried to resuscitate Roscoe & Clarke's bank, and that at
their downfall this picture would in 1833 again figure in the auction
room.

The smelting works and the coal mines at
Bagillt were yet unsold, and were now dealt with
by the assignees.

The liquidation of the bank did not deter
William Stanley Roscoe from matrimony, for
we find that he, on 10th September 1818, at
Audley, co. Stafford, married Hannah Eliza,
eldest daughter of James Caldwell of Linley
Wood, and became resident at Mount Vernon.
William Roscoe had, after leaving Allerton Hall,
gone to live in Rake Lane (now Durning Road),
then for a while resided at 5 St. James's Walk
(now the site of the destined Liverpool Cathedral),
and finally, some time before 1823, took a small
house in Lodge Lane, near the top of Bentley
Road, now numbered 180, and known as Roscoe
House.   Here he, sustained by an annuity which
his friends in Liverpool had purchased on the
joint lives of himself and wife, together with
£100 per annum pension which he received as
"Royal Associate" of the Royal Society of Liter-
ature, passed the remainder of his years in calm
literary and botanical pursuits.   He died on 30th
June 1831, in the seventy-ninth year of his age.

John Clarke did not long survive his bankruptcy.
He died suddenly at Crook Hall, near Wigan,
one of his estates, on 9th August 1821, aged 65.

Prior to his death he had, however, the satisfaction of seeing all liabilities on his personal

estate paid in full, with a good surplus for the
joint estate of the proprietors. The Orrell
colliery, in which he and Roscoe were interested,
on later development became a valuable property,
and materially increased the dividends to the
creditors of the bank.

His coal business was for some time carried on
by Benjamin Frankland as agent for John Clarke,
but in 1823 the style of the firm is Clarke &
Frankland, and as such was in existence for many
years. A small point in the history of the firm,
but one indicative of the character of the
originator, is that during hard winters, when the
cost of bringing coal to Liverpool—viz. by barges
—was considerably increased owing to the frost,
the price of coal was never raised against the small
purchaser. Such a one could buy his coal practically at the same rates as during those months
when the canals were free from ice. This policy,
a subject for political skits at election time, was
initiated by John Clarke, and continued after his
death by Clarke & Frankland.

The author has not been able to ascertain when
or to whom John Clarke was married. His wife's
Christian name was Alice, and they had numerous
children. A daughter was married 22nd October
1822 to Ambrose Lace.[1]

[1] Ambrose Lace was an attorney, in partnership with his father,
Joshua Lace. The latter was Roscoe's partner with Samuel Aspinall

Of the sons, William Dyson Clarke died 1st September 1825, aged 40, and the fourth son, Charles, died 2nd January 1836.

William Roscoe had a numerous progeny. He himself was an only son, and his only sister, Margaret, married Daniel Daulby of Rydal Mount, Westmorland, and died his widow 1st May 1827, aged 72. After him Daulby Street is named.

Of Roscoe's children, the eldest, William Stanley Roscoe, has full separate reference.

Edward, the second son, was an iron merchant, residing in Toxteth Park. His partnership with Crawford Logan was dissolved November 1826, and the firm then became Roscoe & Waln, but by 1829 the title of his firm was Mather, Roscoe, and Co. He died at River Bank, Toxteth Park, on 11th July 1834, in his fiftieth year. His wife Margaret died 28th April 1840, aged 53.

James, the third son, died, aged 41, on 3rd April 1829.

until the dissolution of partnership in September 1792. Joshua Lace by 1802 had taken a partner, Thomas Hassall, their business place being in Union Court. By 1811 this partnership had ceased, Joshua Lace continuing alone. By 1818 the firm had become Lace, Miller, & Lace, the new partners being William Spurstow Miller and Ambrose Lace. By 1832 the firm had divided, Ambrose Lace forming the new firm of Ambrose Lace & Sons, and Miller taking a partner, Lawrence Peel, under the style of Miller & Peel. This, many years later, became Mil'er, Peel, & Hughes, the latest accession being John Hughes, Mayor in 1881-2. The present head of the firm is William Watson Rutherford, M.P., Lord Mayor of Liverpool 1902-3, and the style of the firm has become "Rutherfords."

Richard became a physician (M.D. Edin. 1826), and died on 3rd October 1864 at Humberton, in Leicestershire, aged 71.

Henry became a barrister, and married, 29th October 1831, Maria, second daughter of Thomas Fletcher (see Fletcher, Roscoe, & Co.). He was appointed Judge of the Liverpool Borough Court, was the author of several legal works and of the Life of his father, and died 23rd March 1836, aged 37. His son is the present Sir Henry Roscoe, Professor of Chemistry, of Manchester.

Mary Anne, the eldest daughter, married, 23rd November 1825, Thomas Jevons, iron merchant. She died 13th November 1845, aged 50; and he died at Pisa, 8th November 1855, aged 64, and was buried in the Protestant Cemetery at Leghorn. Their son, William Stanley Jevons, born 1st September 1835, was drowned while bathing on 13th August 1882. His death was a great loss to economic science. He published many valuable scientific works, and had in view a "Treatise on Economics," which he intended as his *magnum opus*. But this remained unwritten.

ROSCOE, CLARKE, WARDELL, & CO.

When the former firm had to meet their creditors in 1816 it was judged prudent to endeavour to conserve the good part of the business. To this end they took into partnership William

Wardell. William Roscoe's note runs : " For the
purpose of separating this from our former concern, and of obtaining additional assistance in our
bank, we are negotiating to take into partnership
a very respectable young man, who was brought
up with us." This new firm lasted till 1820,
when the Roscoes and John Clarke were declared
bankrupt. The firm then became

LOWRY, ROSCOE, & WARDELL.

The new principal of the firm was Thomas
Lowry, who resided and had a brewery in Cunliffe
Street. They removed from the old premises,
No. 1 Castle Street, to 4 Dale Street, nearly
opposite. Both Lowry and Wardell had official
connection with the Liverpool Gas Light Co.;
in 1821 Wardell was Chairman and Lowry
Treasurer.[1] The Roscoe was William Stanley
Roscoe, William Roscoe having definitely
retired.

On 11th September 1826 William Wardell
married, at Grasmere, Elizabeth, daughter of
John Gregory Crump, attorney, Liverpool, and
went to reside in Erskine Street.

By the end of 1827 this partnership terminated, Lowry and Wardell ceasing to be mem-

---

[1] In 1820 the Gas Company was entirely directed by bankers,
Samuel Hope being Chairman, William Wardell, Deputy-Chairman,
and Thomas Lowry, Treasurer.

bers.[1] Wardell went to Chester and joined Messrs. Dixons' Bank, the title becoming Dixons and Wardell, and so continued till his death in 1864.[2] Thomas Lowry, now resident in Rupert Lane, contented himself with his brewery.[3]

Fresh partners and capital had now to be brought into the business. Roscoe opened nego-

[1] One of the clerks of Lowry, Roscoe & Wardell had a brilliant banking career. This was James Lister, son of the Rev. James Lister, Pastor of Lime Street Baptist Chapel. He was with them from 1813 to 1825. In the latter year he joined Cunliffe, Brooks, & Co., of Manchester, with whom he continued until October 1829. He then entered the service of the Manchester and Liverpool District Bank, and in June 1832 the manager at Liverpool, James Baird, having resigned, he was appointed manager *pro tem.* This appointment was, later on, confirmed, and he remained with them until 1835, when, on the formation of the Liverpool Union Bank, he was appointed manager of that bank. He remained so for forty years, becoming, on his retirement, a director of the bank whose career he had managed from its commencement, and whose business had become, during that period, a magnificent monument to his ability.

[2] W. Wardell's wife, Elizabeth, died at Chester on 23rd March 1835. He himself survived till 14th March 1864. From his will, proved at Chester 18th April 1864, he appears to have had no sons, mention being made only of a daughter married to Arthur Potts of Hoole Hall, Chester. The estate was sworn under £80,000. It is to be noted that one of his executors was the above James Lister, the manager of the Liverpool Union Bank. Messrs. Dixons' bank was bought by Parr's Banking Company.

[3] On 13th September 1830 died Ann, wife of Thomas Lowry, in her fifty-third year. The following year, on March 24th, their two daughters were married : Elizabeth, the elder, to Thomas Mann, and Ann, the younger, to James Stringer. By 1832 Thomas Lowry appears to have given up the brewery, and to have joined his son-in-law as merchants, under the style of Lowry, Stringer & Mann. But on 4th February 1833 his son Thomas died in his twenty-fourth year, and by 1837 he himself retired from business, leaving the mercantile firm as "Stringer & Mann." They later on established steam saw-mills in Seel Street.

tiations with John Roberts, a merchant residing
in Rake Lane (now Durning Road), with his
office at 2 Dale Street, and with John Tarleton,
who had been brought up in the bank. Then
Thomas Fletcher, whose partnership in the firm
of Fletcher, Yates, & Co. had just terminated,
approached William Stanley Roscoe, and eventually
a new firm blossomed out under the title of

FLETCHER, ROBERTS, ROSCOE, & Co.

They took offices at 8 High Street, a few
doors away from the old premises in Dale
Street.

Thomas Fletcher at this time was sixty years
old, having been born 22nd June 1767, the eldest
child of John and Hannah Fletcher. The family
were originally yeomen, but both John Fletcher
and his father before him were hatters, largely
in the export trade, in Castle Street, near Swift's
Court.   Thomas Fletcher was apprenticed in
his sixteenth year to James France, an extensive
Jamaica merchant. About the time of the expiry
of Fletcher's six years' apprenticeship James France
withdrew from the firm, leaving a large amount
of capital with them, and his nephew, Thomas
Hayhurst, became the head of the firm.   Fletcher
became the junior partner, bringing in £2000,
which was largely made up of monies borrowed
from the family property.

He married at Norwich, on 1st October 1795, Anne, eldest daughter of Dr. Enfield.[1]

When James France died, 1795, Thomas Hayhurst, in accordance with the terms of the will, assumed the name of France. He also invested, under the terms of the will, a considerable portion of James France's money in real estate, buying Bostock, in Cheshire, where his descendants reside. In 1801 there was a reconstruction of the firm, and Joseph Brooks Yates and John Henry Matthews, both of whom had been for some time with the firm, were taken into partnership. In this new firm Joseph Brooks Yates obtained a quarter share, although just out of his apprenticeship. This was due to his father, the Rev. John Yates,[2] who had a secret interest in the firm. On 8th January 1815 died Thomas France (formerly Hayhurst), and on the reconstruction of the firm Thomas Fletcher became senior, the style now being Fletcher, Yates, & Co. When the last partnership with Joseph Brooks Yates terminated, 31st December 1827, the respective

[1] He was the author of the first history of Liverpool, compiled from the papers of George Perry, and published at Warrington 1773.

[2] Pastor of the Unitarian Chapel in Paradise Street, now the site of the Queen's Theatre. He married, in 1779, Elizabeth, the widow of Dr. Bostock, daughter of John Ashton and sister of Nicholas Ashton. He was a speculative parson, and it is said that he obtained the money, which now put his son at so early an age in such a prominent position, by a fortunate deal in tobacco. Possibly this occurred in 1776, when no tobacco entered Liverpool between May and the end of December.

amounts of capital in the firm were : J. B. Yates three-fifths, and Thomas Fletcher two-fifths. Yates now required Fletcher to bring more capital into the concern, well knowing this to be impossible, and hence Fletcher was practically pushed from the firm. At this time his holding in the books was £18,000, but by depreciation of shipping this was reduced to £11,000.

During his membership of the above firm he did good public service. In 1824 he was one of the six commercial members who, for the first time, were added to the Dock Board. He retained his seat six years. The West India Association was formed in 1799. In 1803 Thomas Fletcher was Vice-Chairman, and in 1806 Chairman of that body.

Now when the negotiations for the new partnerships in the Roscoe Bank came to a head, it was found that the supposed capitalist, John Roberts, was not to be a member of the firm, but in his stead a brother Richard was put forward. He introduced £7500, and Thomas Fletcher a similar amount. Nothing was expected from either William Stanley Roscoe or John Tarleton. Francis Fletcher (son of Thomas), who had been with Fletcher, Yates, & Co. for ten years, was to be cashier as assistant to Tarleton at a salary of £200 a year for seven years, and after that was to be admitted to a partnership. There was a condition that not more than £500 should be advanced to any one person without the consent of the majority of the partners, and, on the suggestion of Thomas Fletcher, Francis Fletcher was at once admitted a partner, taking one-fourth of his father's share. The business they had was worth £3000 a year if properly conducted.

But Roberts' capital turned out to be a delusion. John Roberts had borrowed every shilling of the £7500 from Williams & Co. of Chester. It was placed to the credit of Richard Roberts, but John opened an account at the bank, and by degrees drew the whole amount out in way of loan to himself, and so repaid the Chester Bank their advance. In the words of Thomas Fletcher, " In short, it was what is commonly known as a ' fair take-in.' "

Roberts and Tarleton drew together, the latter marrying, on the 16th July 1830, Jane Ellen, the sister of the former. Roscoe had full faith in Tarleton, the result being that the three sanctioned the loan to John Roberts and other heavy advances. The bank was soon entangled further with John Roberts. He had a slate quarry in Wales, and brought his bills on various agents, employed to sell the slates, to the bank for discount. Further, the Robertses and Tarleton negotiated a partnership for another brother, Robert Roberts, with Robert Rawlinson, timber merchant, of

1 Sefton Street, who had an account with the bank. For this firm also were discounted bills drawn against sales of timber into the country, many of which were found to come back.

Matters progressed in this way until, on 23rd July 1833, Fletcher, Roscoe, & Co. received a letter from their London agents, Jones, Loyd, and Co., announcing that they would no longer accept Fletcher & Co.'s drafts. The next day the bank stopped payment. They held considerable amounts of Customs and Excise money. Writs were at once issued, and the officers of the law laid hands on all property belonging to the partners, jointly and severally, and satisfied their demands.

After a delay of some weeks, and an investigation of affairs, it was resolved to go into bankruptcy, and a fiat was issued on 13th September 1833 against Thomas Fletcher, William Stanley Roscoe, Richard Roberts, John Tarleton, and Francis Fletcher, trading under the firm of Fletcher, Roscoe, Roberts, & Co.

In addition to the Roberts' entanglement the bank had contracted bad debts to a considerable amount, but the chief causes of the catastrophe were the accounts of John Roberts, and Rawlinson & Roberts. The total amount of the liabilities was £30,000, and the concern only realised 5s. in the £.

When, in July, Jones, Loyd, & Co. stopped the account, Fletcher, Roscoe, & Co. had with them a cash advance of £10,000 amply secured by bills. When all these came to maturity, Jones, Loyd, & Co. had to refund £5000 to the receiver of the estate, Harmood Banner. Among Thomas Fletcher's assets were one-fourth interest in a mortgage for £5636, 7s. 10d. on a coffee plantation called Friendship Hall, Portland, Jamaica, with seventy slaves thereon, and one-fourth of a mortgage for £16,000 on the moiety of a sugar estate, called Fellowship Hall, St. Mary's, Jamaica, and of the fifty slaves on the estate.

Thomas Fletcher received his bankruptcy certificate on 2nd September 1834, Francis Fletcher on 3rd October 1834, but that of William Stanley Roscoe was delayed till 8th January 1836.

Thomas Fletcher's friends, both in and out of the family, rallied round him, and subscribed a sum of £2000, which was placed in trust. He retired to a cottage at Gateacre, where he died in 1850. His wife Anna, born 3rd September 1770, died 5th December 1836, in her sixty-seventh year.

Their son Francis, born 15th November 1799, married, 27th October 1831, Marriott, youngest daughter of John Martineau of Stamford Hill, London. After the break-up of the bank he went to reside with his father-in-law, and later obtained a place in the Poor Law Commissioner's office.

Maria, second daughter of Thomas Fletcher, was married to Henry Roscoe 29th October 1831, and was the mother of the present Sir Henry Roscoe of Manchester.

The third daughter, Emily, was married to Charles Booth on 20th August 1829; and the fourth, Caroline, to Charles Crompton on 20th March 1832.

Of the Robertses all trace is lost, but their brother-in-law, John Tarleton, became the manager at Cork of the Agricultural and Commercial Bank of Ireland.

William Stanley Roscoe, during the winding-up of the bank, published in 1834 a book of "Poems," and possibly this, his second bankruptcy, had a little to do with the following sonnet :—

To the Harvest Moon

"Again thou reignest in thy golden hall,
  Rejoicing in thy sway, fair queen of night !
  The ruddy reapers hail thee with delight,
Theirs is the harvest, theirs the joyous call
For tasks well ended ere the season's fall.
  Sweet orb, thou smilest from thy starry height,
  But whilst on them thy beams are shedding bright,
To me thou com'st o'ershadow'd with a pall :

To me alone the year hath fruitless flown,
  Earth hath fulfill'd her trust through all her lands,
The good man gathereth where he hath sown,
  And the great master in his vineyard stands ;
But I, as if my task were all unknown,
  Come to his gates, alas, with empty hands."

He was appointed Sergeant of Mace to the
Liverpool Corporation, a position which, under
the Reformed Municipality, carried a salary of
£350 per annum. He died 31st October 1843,
aged 61. His wife survived him till 15th
February 1854, being then aged 68. Their
son, William Caldwell Roscoe, writer of some
promising verse, was born 20th September 1823,
and died 30th July 1859.

Whatever dire results to the peace and fortune
of William Roscoe were brought about by his
endeavour to rescue the firm of Clarkes from
their embarrassments at the close of the eighteenth
century, their descendants later on were loyal to
him, and, so far as lay in their power, endeavoured to remove the stigma of bankruptcy from
his honoured name. The Clarkes in the course
of time became possessed of means, of which they
made commendable use in providing a substantial
further dividend (eight had already been paid)
on the liabilities of the old banking firm of
Roscoe, Clarke, & Roscoe. The creditors thereupon unanimously consented to an annulment of

the bankruptcy. When De Quincey in 1837 wrote " Mr. Roscoe is dead, and has found time to be half forgotten," he did not reckon on the kindly human feeling, quite unknown to him, which William Roscoe had inspired in his friends. The late Joseph Mayer, an artist to the finger-tips, repeatedly pointed out the value of William Roscoe's influence, and the citizens of Liverpool of to-day have recognised this by associating his name with the Chair of Architecture and Applied Art founded in 1881 in the Victoria University, now the University of Liverpool.

Recurring to the annulment of bankruptcy, we find that on 2nd and 30th November and 3rd December 1843 meetings of the creditors in the bank were held before Mr. Commissioner Phillips for the purpose of their voting upon the accept-ance of a composition offered by the family of the late John Clarke in order to a final examina-tion and supersedeas of the bankruptcy. The creditors at the three meetings unanimously voted acceptance. The debts proved amounted to £204,000, and creditors were 578 in number. The Commissioner, on careful consideration of all the facts, found that the statutory requisi-tions, secs. 133 and 134, 6 George IV., and the order of Lord Eldon of 27th June 1826, had been strictly complied with. It therefore became his duty to transmit the proceedings to the Court of Review for its sanction. He hoped, however, it would not be out of place if he expressed the pleasure with which he performed this duty. The name of Roscoe was inseparably connected with that of Liverpool, the scene of his nativity. Most happy was he therefore that, in strict accordance with his duty, an act should have become his, the more gratifying to himself, because grateful to a town which derived a noble distinction from this great man's memory.

What gives cause for surprise is that Picton, who surely must have known well how the influence of William Roscoe extended far beyond his day and generation, has made no mention of this graceful and grateful act of expiation.

CHAPTER VI

CHARLES CALDWELL AND CO.

Charles Caldwell & Co.—Partners—War of the French Revolution—
Bankruptcy of the firm—Great fall in Consols and cotton—Thomas
Smyth's sons—Renewal of the commission of bankruptcy in 1832.

THE first mention of this firm is in the appendix
to the directory of 1774. The partners were
Thomas Smyth and Charles Caldwell. Thomas
Smyth was a merchant whose place of business
and residence were in Paradise Street, the bank
being carried on in an adjoining building. At
this date Thomas Smyth had made himself a
name as a successful merchant. This year, and
for many successive years, his name appears as
elected to the Chamber of Commerce. He was
selected as a member of the Common Council of
Liverpool on 3rd April 1782, was elected bailiff
in October of the same year, and became Mayor
in 1789. His country house was Fairview, Toxteth Park, beautifully situated on the crest of the
hill, where now runs High Park Street.

Charles Caldwell was a merchant who, according to the Poll Book of 1761, lived in Lord
Street, but by 1774 was resident in the pleasant

country district of Bevington Bush (alas, how
changed!), and by 1781 had removed to St.
James's Street. I believe, but have no direct evidence, that he was a partner in Oldham, Caldwell,
and Co., whose transactions were principally in
sugar. He figured largely in Liverpool society,
and acted occasionally, in conjunction with our
best local gentry, as steward for the races at
Crosby. The banking firm came directly into
evidence in this year, 1774, for they were
appointed in the *Gazette* of 30th July one of
the receivers of light gold, for which proper-
weight coins were issued in return.

Matters appear to have gone smoothly with
the firm, Thomas Smyth being regarded as one
of the principal merchants of the town, until the
outbreak of the war with France in 1793. Their
London agents were Burton, Forbes, & Gregory.
This firm, under the title of Forbes & Gregory,
of Aldermanbury, London, was gazetted on 19th
March, and that of Charles Caldwell & Co. followed on 30th March. From the *Gazette* notice
of the latter failure it would appear that the
London agents had more than an agent's interest
in the firm, that, in fact, they were partners.

Business had been booming for some years past
in Liverpool; shipping and cotton especially had
increased their volume, and with this increase
came steadily rising prices. The outbreak of

war caused a rapid fall. In cotton alone the drop
was from 6d. to 7d. per lb. Consols dropped
to 70½, the highest point of the preceding year
having been 97. The shipping of Liverpool
had increased largely. The average annual
tonnage for the seven years ending 1786 was
151,347; for the next seven years the average
was 260,380 tons. The importation of cotton
was on a rapidly increasing scale. For 1790 the
imports into Liverpool were 9,608,741 pounds;
for 1791, 12,198,805 pounds; and for 1792,
14,064,573 pounds. There was thus a considerable accumulation of stocks. Charles Caldwell
and Co. and several of their clients[1] held large
quantities of cotton, and hence suffered badly
from the enormous drop in the market value
of the staple. The assignees of Charles Caldwell
and Co. were Richard Walker, John Bolton, and
Thomas Leyland,[2] and they set to work at once

[1] Among the clients of C. Caldwell & Co. was the firm of Browne,
Brown, & Co., the senior of whom was the father of Felicia Dorothea
Browne, afterwards Mrs. Hemans. Browne & Brown were extensive
holders of cotton, and came to grief. The assets of the firm, and the
furniture and residences of the partners, were sold by auction. At the
very time the Brownes were removing their remaining furniture from
their house in Duke Street the future Mrs. Hemans was born, and
her infelicitous arrival was a source of inconvenience to the incoming
owner, Cornelius Bourne.

[2] The three assignees were perhaps the wealthiest men in Liver-
pool. For Richard Walker, see under Gregson & Co.; for John
Bolton, under Staniforth & Co.; and or Thomas Leyland, under
Leyland & Bullins.

to realise the assets. They ordered the public
sale of the stocks of Jamaica sugar, London re-
fined sugar, West India cotton and Pernambuco
cotton. They also on 11th June sold the furniture, &c., of Thomas Smyth's house, Fairview.
There were prints, a large amount of plate,
and "the finest wines, brandy, and rum, perhaps,
in the country." On the same date were sold
the contents of the Paradise Street premises. On
24th June was sold the furniture of Charles
Caldwell, at his house in St. James's Street.

There was a great deal of litigation about
the estate, including one suit as to whether the
proceeds of the realisation should be banked
with the Bank of England or with a private
bank. But there was no attempt to resume
business.

Charles Caldwell for a while resided in St.
Anne's Street, but some time before 1803 went
to reside at 7 Bold Street, where he died 10th
January 1814, aged 75.

Thomas Smyth does not appear to have remained in Liverpool after the ruin of his business, although his name appears in the list of
Aldermen up to 1811. He died at The Fence,
Macclesfield, on 12th July 1824, in the eighty-
seventh year of his age.

His son, William Smyth, born in Liverpool in
1765, went to Eton and Cambridge, where he

graduated eighth Wrangler, was elected a Fellow
of his College, Peterhouse, proceeding to M.A.
in 1790. The failure of the bank in 1793
caused him to look out for employment, and
he became tutor to Richard Brinsley Sheridan's
elder son, Thomas. He found the general difficulty of extracting any money from Sheridan,
and he records that on one occasion when taking
his pupil to London, instead of coin for defray-
ing their expenses, they were given orders on
Drury Lane. Later he obtained a tutorship at
Peterhouse, and in 1807 was appointed Regius
Professor of Modern History at Cambridge,
which office he retained till his death. On the
death of his father in 1824 he inherited real
property, and on that account, under the then
rules of the College, his Fellowship was declared
vacant. He died unmarried, 24th June 1849,
at Norwich, and was buried in the Cathedral,
a stained-glass window to his memory being
erected over the grave.

There is now in the hall of Peterhouse a portrait of William Smyth, presented by his brother,
the Rev. Thomas Smyth (1778–1854), Fellow of
Oriel College, Oxford.

The above particulars of the sons are taken
from the " Dictionary of National Biography."

A third brother was Edward, who lived at The
Fence, Macclesfield.

Mr. Earwaker, "East Cheshire," vol. ii. 454, London, 1880, says :—

"This township (Hurdsfield) consists almost entirely of copyhold estates, held under the manor and forest of Macclesfield. . . . The Fence, an old house in this township, was in the latter part of the seventeenth century in possession of a family named Holland, of whom there is frequent mention in the Macclesfield and other registers. In 1765 it was the residence of Harry Langford, and appears at that time, or shortly afterwards, to have been in the possession of the Smyth family. In 1804, Thomas Smyth was living there, and subsequently, I believe, his son, Edward Smyth, Esq. It was for many years the residence of the late Thomas Brocklehurst, Esq., and was purchased by him from Colonel Smyth in 1869."

During the mayoralty of Thomas Smyth his daughter was married, 24th May 1790, at Childwall, to John Johnson, of London.

There was at this period great laxity in administering bankrupt estates. The evil was real, and at length reached such a pitch that an Act, 6th of George IV., entitled "An Act to amend the law relating to Bankruptcy," was passed, with the intent of expediting the closing of long-open accounts, and the consequent distributing of dividends to much-enduring creditors. Under this Act there was a notice of renewed commission of bankruptcy, dated 1st December 1832, "against

Charles Caldwell and Thomas Smyth, both of
Liverpool, and John Forbes and Daniel Gregory,
of London (carrying on business at Liverpool
under the name, style, or firm of Charles Caldwell & Co.)"—poor men, all of them long since
dead—and the commissioners were to meet to
audit the accounts, and to declare a dividend. A
later notice kindly stated that it was necessary to
produce the bills, Probates of Wills, and Letters
of Administration. Be it noted that this was
only forty years after the original default.[1]

[1] There was even a lengthier interval in recent years between the
default and a dividend. On 25th June 1903 there was a sitting at
the County Court, Manchester, to declare a dividend on the estate of
Daintry, Ryle, & Co., bankers, who became bankrupt 7th July 1841
—an interval of sixty-two years. Ryle was father of John C. Ryle,
first Bishop of Liverpool.

CHAPTER VII

ARTHUR HEYWOOD, SONS, AND CO.

Arthur Heywood, Sons, & Co.—Origin of the Heywoods—Transition
from merchants to bankers—Open a branch at Manchester, but
soon close it—Widening of Castle Street, and rebuilding of bank
premises—Samuel Thompson—Building of Brunswick Street
premises—Hugh Jones—Transfer of Corporation accounts to
Heywood's Bank—Samuel Henry Thompson—His sons, Rev.
S. A. Thompson-Yates and Henry Yates Thompson—Sale of the
business to the Bank of Liverpool—Pedigree of the Heywoods.

THIS celebrated banking house had a much
longer lease of life than any other similar firm
in Liverpool. Launched as a separate concern
in 1773, it endured as a private bank until 1883,
when it was purchased by the Bank of Liverpool.

A compact account of the family origin is
given by Picton ("Memorials of Liverpool,"
vol. ii. 17, ed. 1875):—

"The Heywoods come of a sturdy Nonconformist
stock. The Rev. Oliver Heywood of Halifax, a divine
somewhat celebrated in his day, and his brother,
Nathaniel, Vicar of Ormskirk,[1] were both ejected from

[1] In 1859 John Pemberton Heywood placed a new east window in
the chancel of Ormskirk Church in memory of his ancestor, Nathaniel
Heywood.

their livings by the Act of Uniformity in 1662. Nathaniel
had two sons, one bearing his own name, and the other
named Richard. Richard emigrated to Drogheda, and
carried on business as a merchant there. Having no
children, he invited his nephew, Benjamin, son of
Nathaniel, then about twelve years old, to reside with
him as his adopted son. Accordingly he went, and, after
being initiated by him into the art and mystery of the
merchant's craft, in due time succeeded to a thriving
business. He married Anne Graham, the daughter of
General Arthur Graham of Armagh, and niece to the
then Mayor of Drogheda, through whom he inherited
landed estates in Ireland, still in possession of the family.
He died in 1725, in the thirty-eighth year of his age,
leaving a large fortune to his family. The widow proved
herself a very Cornelia to his children, refusing all offers
of marriage, and devoting herself entirely to their welfare. The two sons were named Arthur and Benjamin.
Arthur came to Liverpool in 1731, and served an
apprenticeship of five years to John Hardman of Allerton
Hall, elected M.P. for the borough in 1754. Benjamin
came ten years later, in 1741, and was bound apprentice
to James Crosby (Mayor in 1753)."

Arthur Heywood at first had his business
premises and residence in Lord Street, and is
described of that address in an advertisement
in Williamson's *Advertiser* for 1758. The Poll
Book of 1761 also gives him as of Lord Street.
But the earliest directory, 1766, contains the
entry: "Arthur and Benjamin Heywood, merchants, Hanover Street." They had built them

houses side by side (Nos. 58 and 59) in 1774, on the east side of Hanover Street, between Seel Street and Gradwell Street, and immediately behind their property was a tennis court. The bank, as such, is not mentioned in the directory of 1774, but doubtless various traders and private persons had, as was the custom in those days, entrusted their accumulations to the responsible merchants, and the time was now ripe for the emergence of the bank from the double part of merchant and financial agent. This change was brought prominently before the public by the appointment, in a supplement dated 1st July 1774 to the Royal Proclamation of 24th June 1774, of A. and B. Heywood as the persons in Liverpool authorised to receive the light gold then in circulation, and to exchange for it gold of full weight. It is a matter to be noted that the various proclamations, which named representative firms in all parts of the kingdom, in no case describe them as bankers. That distinctive appellation is reserved for the Bank of England.

Needless to say, this singling out of Messrs. Heywood perturbed others in the town, who rightly considered that they had some claim to be considered. Hence C. Caldwell & Co., who appear as bankers in the appendix of the local directory of 1774, intimate that they are also appointed, as notified in the *Gazette* of 30th July,

receivers of the gold coin. Similarly, Samuel
Warren, goldsmith, 11 Castle Street, intimates
that he also has been appointed a receiver. It is
interesting to observe that Heywoods, although
they are not in any official list of bankers, yet
date their public circular from " Bank, Liverpool," giving no other address, although the
place is given in the body of the notice :—

"BANK, LIVERPOOL, 12th July 1774.

" His Majesty having been pleased to appoint US for
this place to receive the diminished Gold Coin of the
Realm, and to exchange the same, agreeable to His
Royal Proclamation of 15th June last . . . We do
hereby give notice that attendance will be given for that
Purpose at our Office, No. 59 Hanover Street, from and
after the 15th July to the 31st August next (inclusive)
between the Hours of Ten O'clock in the Morning and
One in the Afternoon, and betwixt Four and Six in the
Afternoon every Wednesday and Saturday, for People
from the Country, and Towns People possessed of small
Sums, and every Monday, Tuesday, and Friday for the
other Inhabitants.

"ARTHUR HEYWOOD, SON, & Co."

Having thus introduced Arthur Heywood on
his public career, it is desirable that we should
hark back to consider him in his private capacity.
We also notice the parting of the brothers, both
of them quitting the career of merchants for that
of bankers.

ARTHUR HEYWOOD

In 1739, being then twenty-two years of age, Arthur Heywood married Elizabeth, daughter of Samuel Ogden of Mossley Hill, Liverpool, and Penelope, his wife, daughter and co-heiress of John Pemberton, a burgess of Chester, who had amassed a large fortune as a Liverpool merchant. John Pemberton had also a daughter Bridget, who married Richard Milnes of Wakefield. They had several children, one being named Hannah.[1]

Elizabeth Heywood died 8th February 1748, leaving a daughter as the issue of the marriage.

On 26th April 1750 Arthur Heywood married the above-mentioned Hannah Milnes.[2]

In 1751 Benjamin Heywood married Phœbe, the sister of Arthur's first wife.

The two brothers were successful in business. They had their experience of the African trade, dabbled a little in privateering, having their Letters of Marque; were recognised as representative merchants, and as such were elected to the Chamber of Commerce.

The change from merchant to banker in the case of Arthur Heywood took place in 1773, he

[1] From another child of Richard and Bridget Milnes came, as grandson, Richard Monckton Milnes, Lord Houghton.

[2] An advertisement of 28th May 1756 indicates part of the property which Richard Milnes came into by marriage with John Pemberton's daughter: "To be Lett a new Large House and Warehouse in Fenwick Street, near Dry Bridge, belonging to Mr. R. Milnes of Wakefield. Enquire of Mr. Arthur Heywood." Either this, or property contiguous to it, became in 1798 the site of Heywood's Bank.

being then fifty-five years of age. When a second notice relative to the " diminished gold " appeared on 11th April 1776, it was stated that operations were conducted " *at the Bank in Castle Street*," also at Arthur Heywood's office in Hanover Street. A curious feature of this second notice is that Heywoods were not content to exchange the gold merely at those addresses, but certain specified dates were given on which they would visit Prescot, Warrington, and Ormskirk for the convenience of the country districts.

When the bank was established in Castle Street, then a narrow street only 18 feet wide, Richard, the eldest son of Arthur, took up his residence on the bank premises, as was the usual custom. On 25th May 1781 he married Mary, the daughter of William Earle of Redcross Street. In 1784 Arthur Heywood, Sons, & Co. opened a branch at Manchester under the management of Richard Ogden. The latter not proving a success, in 1786 Arthur Heywood took over the management, but after six months' experience of it closed the branch.

Benjamin Heywood had two sons, Benjamin Arthur and Nathaniel, residing with him in Hanover Street. Benjamin Arthur was in business in Chorley Street, Liverpool, under the title of Parke & Heywood, also in Lancaster as Parke, Heywood, & Conway. The latter firm was

HEYWOOD'S BANK, CASTLE STREET, 1787

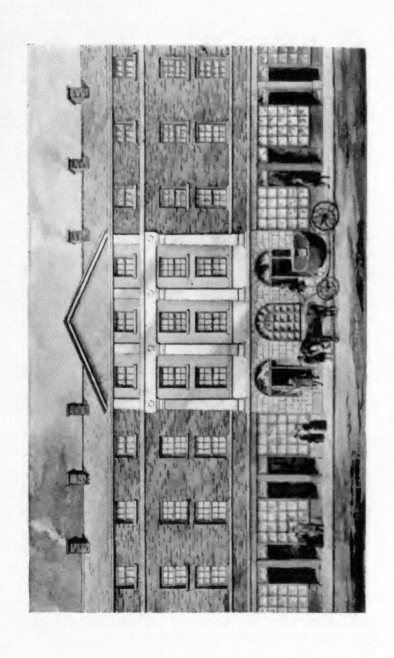

dissolved in May 1785. They dealt in African goods, ivory, &c., and had privateers, but their staple trade was linen. The senior was Thomas Parke (see Gregson & Co.).

In 1788 Benjamin Arthur and Nathaniel, being then aged thirty-three and twenty-eight years respectively, proceeded to Manchester, and, with their father as senior, on 26th May commenced business as bankers. They founded a great business.

Some time before 1785 Richard Heywood had acquired, and was resident at, Lark Hill, West Derby, still in possession of descendants of the Heywoods, and his place in the bank house was taken by Arthur Heywood, junior.

In 1786 the west side of Castle Street was taken down, and the street carried back to its present alignment, Brunswick Street being opened at the same time. This necessitated the entire rebuilding of the bank premises.

When the mighty financial crash came in 1793 Heywoods' stood firm, and supported the measures taken for the maintenance of credit.

Shortly afterwards there was an accession to the firm of a new member, Samuel Thompson. He had been in their employ for some time. In the directory for 1796 he appears in the appendix under the head of "Heywood & Thompson, merchants," but not till 1800 is he mentioned as banker.

G

On 11th February 1795 died Arthur Heywood, the founder of the firm, being then in his seventy-ninth year, and on 10th August of the same year his brother, and long time partner, Benjamin, died at Manchester, aged 72.[1]

In 1798 the Heywoods began the construction of the building—which is still associated with their name — the bank premises in Brunswick Street, with dwelling-house attached, having entrance from Fenwick Street.

The date of removal from Castle Street to Brunswick Street is approximately given in the following advertisement of January 1799 :—

" To be sold all those buildings on the west side of Higher Castle Street, now used in part as a bank by Messrs. Heywood & Co., and in part as a dwelling-house with coach-house behind. Possession may be had in May 1800, or sooner if the new bank, building by Messrs. Heywoods in Brunswick Street, shall be ready for occupation." [2]

On 3rd May 1800 Richard Heywood died, aged 49, at his seat at Lark Hill, "a gentleman universally respected for his integrity, benevolence,

---

1 Arthur Heywood's widow, Hannah, survived him till 8th September 1806, dying at her then residence, 4 Great George Street, at the age of 83. Benjamin's widow, Phœbe, removed to 16 Knight Street, where she died 25th May 1810, aged 84.

2 The building in Castle Street was taken down in 1864 to make way for the new building of the Mercantile and Exchange Bank, which had a short and inglorious career. It is now occupied by the Scottish Widows Insurance Company.

HUGH JONES

and goodness of heart." He had no children,[1] and
the headship of the bank devolved on his younger
brother Arthur (II).

The partner, Samuel Thompson, had in 1800
his residence at 48 School Lane, but on 13th
August 1801 he married Miss Hughes, the
daughter of John Hughes, Esq., of Chester,
and took a house in the more fashionable quarter of Slater Street, where he resided till about
1806–7, when he removed to Rodney Street.

The fourth son of Arthur (I) was John
Pemberton Heywood, a barrister, who resided
at Wakefield. Two of his sons, Richard (II)
and John Pemberton (II), became members of
the banking firm.

The second son of Arthur (I) was Benjamin
(III), who resided at Stanley Hall, Wakefield.
He had married Elizabeth, the widow of William
Serjeantson. Their eldest daughter, Elizabeth,
married on 24th March 1806, at St. Thomas's
Church, Liverpool, Hugh Jones.

Hugh Jones was the youngest son of Thomas
Jones (1740–99) of The Court, Wrexham, son
of John Jones, who had married Maria Mar-
garetta, daughter and co-heir of Sir Thomas
Longueville, Bart. Thomas Jones was formerly
Lieutenant in the 104th Foot, and subsequently

[1] His widow, Mary, died 11th December 1831, in her seventy-fifth
year, at her house in St. Michael's, Toxteth Park.

Captain of Militia, both of Denbighshire and
Merionethshire. He had married, first, Jane
Jones; secondly, Ann Lloyd, and Hugh Jones
was an offspring of the second marriage. The
latter was born 20th September 1777. His
eldest brother, Thomas Longueville Jones, took
by Royal Licence the name of Longueville in
lieu of that of Jones, and was the progenitor
of the family of Longuevilles of Oswestry. On
his marriage, Hugh Jones became a partner in
Heywoods' Bank, and took up his residence at
8 Great George Square, but by 1813 he had
taken a house, No. 61, in the chosen retreat
of the affluent and dignified, Rodney Street.

On 24th September 1822 died at his seat,
Stanley Hall, Wakefield, Benjamin Heywood,
aged 70. He was succeeded at Stanley Hall
by his son Arthur (III), who married, 1st
June 1825, Mary Duroure. He died *s.p.* in
1831.

On 16th December 1833 died in his thirty-
second year another member of the firm, Richard
(II), son of John Pemberton Heywood of Wakefield.

The year 1835 marks the transference of the
entire Corporation accounts to Heywoods' Bank,
thus adding further prestige to the firm. Fuller
note of the matter is given under Leyland and
Bullins. The following year saw many events

SAMUEL HENRY THOMPSON

which had influence on the proprietorship of the bank.

On the 9th January, at his house in Abercromby Square, died Samuel Thompson,[1] in his sixty-ninth year. He was succeeded in the bank by his son, Samuel Henry Thompson, who married, 24th January 1837, Elizabeth, eldest daughter of Joseph Brooks Yates of West Dingle.

On 28th January 1836, at St. George's Church, Liverpool, was married Robertson Gladstone, second son of John Gladstone[2] of Liverpool, and Fasque, Kincardineshire, to Mary Ellen, third daughter of Hugh Jones, a partner in Heywoods'. In the fulness of time their son, Robertson Gladstone, obtained a partnership in the bank.

[1] In addition to his partnership in the bank, Samuel Thompson had a subsidiary business as insurance broker, jointly with William Thompson, junior, James Thompson, junior, and John Gunning. This partnership was, however, dissolved 31st December 1824, and Samuel Thompson in 1825 opened an insurance office on his own account at 10 Exchange Alley. On 1st November 1826 he was elected a member of the Corporation, and became Bailiff for 1828. His eldest daughter was married at St. Michael's Church, Liverpool, on 6th August 1829 to Owen Wynne of Sligo, eldest son of William Wynne, Esq., of Dublin; and his second son, Arthur, was married at the Parish Church, Prendergast, on 10th September 1836, to Frances Catherine, eldest daughter of James Bellairs, Esq., of The Mount, Haverfordwest.

[2] It is worthy of note that in Billinge's *Liverpool Advertiser* for 1800 appears a single-line entry, " 29th April, John Gladstone, Esq., to Miss Robertson." Two of the sons of that marriage were the above Robertson Gladstone, and William Ewart Gladstone, of world-wide fame.

On 21st April was married at St. George's Church, Liverpool, John Pemberton Heywood, third son of the late John Pemberton Heywood of Wakefield, to Anna Maria, second daughter of the above Hugh Jones. This marriage between close relatives certainly consolidated the several interests in the bank.

On 13th September of the same year died Arthur Heywood (II), in the eighty-third year of his age.[1]

On 11th October was married at Ambleside Richard Heywood, eldest son of Hugh Jones, to Margaret, only daughter of John Harrison, Esq., of Ambleside. He appears to have been given a partnership in the bank a little earlier than this.

Taking leave of the bank in 1837, we find the existing partners are Hugh Jones, his son Richard Heywood Jones, John Pemberton Heywood, and Samuel Henry Thompson.

After the death of Arthur Heywood, Hugh Jones succeeded him in the occupancy of Lark Hill, West Derby, where Arthur Heywood Jones

---

[1] There is no mention of his marriage in any official account, but in "The Creevey Papers," under date 23rd November 1833, Thomas Creevey writes that Arthur Heywood had married what is known in current slang as "a woman of no importance." He mentions a kindness done by Arthur Heywood to a son of the Earl of Sefton, who had committed a similar imprudence, and adds, as to Arthur Heywood's wife, "As she was a remarkably good kind of woman, he may think that Berkeley's tit may be the same" (vol. ii. p. 268, edition 1904).

JOHN PEMBERTON HEYWOOD

still resides. He died, 27th June 1842, at Connaught Place West, Hyde Park, in his sixty-sixth year.[1]

John Pemberton Heywood resided at the bank house in Fenwick Street, but a little later than this period had his country residence at Norris Green, West Derby. He died *s.p.* in 1877.

Samuel Henry Thompson[2] resided with his father in Abercromby Square, but on his marriage he removed to Dingle Cottage, Toxteth, near the home of his wife's relatives. In 1847 he purchased Thingwall Hall, near Liverpool, with about 300 acres of park land. He died December 1892, aged 85.

The banking business was sold in 1883 to the

---

[1] In a notice of his death in the *Liverpool Mercury* occurs the following:—"It would be difficult to name a single benevolent institution which has not experienced his generosity, and will not suffer by his death." He left £500 to the Liverpool Infirmary, and £500 to the Dispensaries.

[2] No account of this bank would be complete without grateful reference to the benefactions which the city of Liverpool has received from this gentleman's sons, Rev. Samuel Ashton Thompson-Yates and Henry Yates Thompson. To the former, who died November 1903, Liverpool University is indebted for its magnificently equipped medical laboratories. To the latter, whom Liverpool delighted to honour in October 1901 by conferring on him the honorary freedom of the city, Liverpool owes its splendid palm-houses in Sefton and Stanley Parks, with adequate furniture. In another direction he is remarkable as having been the proprietor of the *Pall Mall Gazette*, during which period James Greenwood and John Morley were successive editors. He was also the purchaser of the magnificent Ashburnham collection of manuscripts, and the library of Newnham College owes much to his generosity.

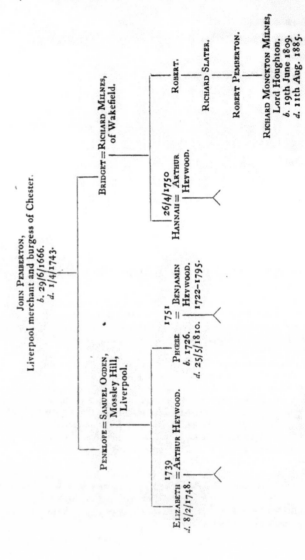

JOHN PEMBERTON,
Liverpool merchant and burgess of Chester.
b. 29/6/1666.
d. 1/4/1743.

PENELOPE = SAMUEL OGDEN,
Mossley Hill,
Liverpool.

BRIDGET = RICHARD MILNES,
of Wakefield.

ELIZABETH = ARTHUR HEYWOOD.
d. 8/2/1748.
1739

PHŒBE = BENJAMIN
b. 1726.   HEYWOOD.
d. 25/5/1810.   1722–1795.
1751

HANNAH = ARTHUR
HEYWOOD.
26/4/1750

ROBERT.

RICHARD SLATER.

ROBERT PEMBERTON.

RICHARD MONCKTON MILNES,
Lord Houghton.
b. 19th June 1809.
d. 11th Aug. 1885.

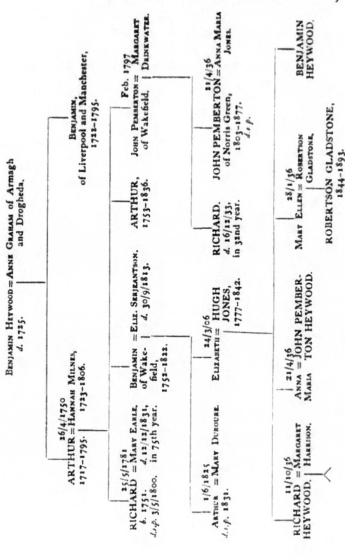

BENJAMIN HEYWOOD = ANNE GRAHAM of Armagh
d. 1725.   and Drogheda.

BENJAMIN,
of Liverpool and Manchester,
1712–1795.

ARTHUR = HANNAH MILNE,
1717–1795.   1723–1806.
        26/4/1750

RICHARD = MARY EARLE,
b. 1751.   d. 12/12/1831,
d.s.p. 3/5/1800.   in 75th year.
        25/5/1781

ARTHUR = ELIZ. SERJEANTSON.
of Wake-   d. 30/9/1813.
field,
1752–1822.

ARTHUR,
1753–1836.

Feb. 1797
JOHN PEMBERTON = MARGARET
of Wakefield.   DARKWATER.

ELIZABETH = HUGH
MARIA   JONES,
        1777–1842.
        24/3/06

ARTHUR = MARY DUROURE.
d.s.p. 1831.
        1/6/1825

RICHARD.
d. 16/12/33,
in 32nd year.

JOHN PEMBERTON = ANNA MARIA
of Norris Green,   JONES.
1803–1877.
d.s.p.
        11/4/36

ANNA = JOHN PEMBER-
MARIA   TON HEYWOOD.
        21/4/36

RICHARD = MARGARET
HEYWOOD.   HARRISON.
        11/10/35

MARY ELLEN = ROBERTSON
            GLADSTONE,
        28/1/36

BENJAMIN
HEYWOOD.

ROBERTSON GLADSTONE,
1844–1893.

Those marked in large type, e.g. ARTHUR, were partners in the firm of Arthur Heywood, Sons, & Co.

Bank of Liverpool for £400,000, and is known
now as the Heywoods' branch of the Bank of
Liverpool.

For convenience of reference, outline pedigrees
are given on pages 104–105.

CHAPTER VIII

WM. GREGSON, SONS, PARKE, AND MORLAND.

THE earliest records of this house commence
during the period of the Seven Years' War with
France.   Privateering was practised by both
nations, and Liverpool contributed its quota of
armed merchantmen.   Among others we find,
in 1756, Messrs. Gregson & Bridge trading with
the West Indies in an armed vessel, and in the
following year despatching a frigate of eighteen
guns.   The senior of the above firm of merchants, and of the subsequent banking firm, was
William Gregson, son of John Gregson.   The
latter died 21st July 1758, in the eighty-third
year of his age, and at that time William Gregson,
in his fortieth year, was already an eminent merchant.   Like other merchants of the period, he
did not confine his activities to one line of
business.   In addition to his mercantile (which

included the African or slave trade), shipowning, and privateering pursuits, Mr. Gregson had a rope-walk, and was an insurance broker, or under-writer, as we should at present term it. The style of the mercantile firm was Gregson and Bridge, subsequently Gregson, Bridge, & Holme. There were two insurance-broking firms with which he was identified—Gregson, Case, & Co., and Gregson, Bridge, & Co. Both these latter firms appear to have dissolved partnership in 1778–9. One circular is as follows :—

" 1st January 1779.

"The partnership carried on between the subscribers, as insurance brokers, under the style or firm of Gregson, Bridge, & Co., is this day dissolved by mutual consent. Persons owing money are requested to pay their debts to Thomas Morland, their clerk, at the office near the Exchange.

WM. GREGSON.
JAMES BRIDGE.[1]
THOS. EARLE.
THOS. BIRCH.[3]

---

[1] James Bridge was Bailiff in 1765. He died 15th December 1791. His widow, Mary, survived him till 2nd July 1835, being then aged 91.

[2] The above Thomas Earle was probably Thomas Earle, afterwards of Spekelands, born 1754, who married his cousin Maria, daughter of Thomas Earle of Leghorn, 20th April 1786, and died 9th July 1822. Through them the Earle family is continued to the present day.

[3] Thomas Birch was Bailiff in 1771, and Mayor in 1777. He was son of Caleb Birch of Whitehaven ; he married Eleanor, daughter of Bernard Bushby, and died in 1782. His son Joseph was partner

We learn from a further circular in 1782 that the firm of Gregson, Case, & Co. was dissolved about the same time as Gregson, Bridge, & Co. This dissolution arose from the bankruptcy of Thomas Case, who was also a partner in the bankrupt firm of Clayton, Case, & Co.

William Gregson took an active interest in the general affairs of Liverpool, was elected 2nd April 1760 a member of the exceedingly "close" Common Council, progressed to Bailiff in the same year, and became Mayor in 1762 (not 1769 as given by Picton). On 17th July 1769 he was sworn Justice of the Peace for the county of Lancaster. In 1761 William Gregson was resident in James Street, but he was one of the earliest merchants to reside in the outskirts of the town. So early as 1769 we find him occupying a house on the east side of the lane leading from Newsham House to Breck Lane. This house was afterwards tenanted by Christopher Rawdon, who in later years was the first Chairman of Directors of the Liverpool Commercial Bank. But in 1786 William Gregson bought and rebuilt

with his father as Liverpool merchants. Born 17th June 1755, he married 6th March 1786 Elizabeth Mary, third daughter of Benjamin Heywood, was for some time M.P. for Nottingham, was created a baronet 30th September 1831, and died 22nd August 1833. His son, Sir Thomas Bernard Birch, Bart., born 18th March 1791, was M.P. for Liverpool 1847–52. Joseph Birch bought the estate of Red Hazles, Prescot, from the Case family, for whom see under Moss and Co.

the house at the corner of Folly Lane (now
Brunswick Road) and Everton Road. This
house had been formerly tenanted by Dr. Fabius,
and subsequently by the father of Joseph Johnson, partner with John Gore in Gore's *Advertiser*.
In front of the grounds was a public well, and
the site is now approximately indicated by the
hostelry known as " Gregson's Well."

Just when the banking firm, as such, crystal-
lised out from the mixture with other businesses
is not clear. The earliest mention of it in the
Liverpool directories is in the year 1790, when
it is given, "William Gregson, Sons, Parke, and
Morland, bankers, 15–16 Paradise Street," near
the lower end of College Lane. They do not
appear in the joint circular of the bankers in June
1784 (see Chapter III.), but the newspapers of
1788 and 1789 make references which indicate
the existence of the bank as a separate institution.
Hence it is considered that it emerged about the
time William Gregson entered his new house, say
1785–6.

The sons in the bank were John and James.
An elder brother, William, was appointed, 2nd
August 1780, Town Clerk of Liverpool, on the
death of Francis Gildart, but died in February
of the following year on his passage to Lisbon,
whither he was proceeding for the benefit of his
health.

The youngest brother, Richard, died 3rd February 1786.

William Gregson also had a daughter, who was married 31st December 1783 to George Case.[1]

At the time of the public appearance of the bank, John Gregson was an Alderman of Liverpool, having been elected Bailiff in 1777, and Mayor in 1784. He resided in Duke Street, at the corner of Suffolk Street, and married, 10th May 1786, Miss Clay, daughter of the late Richard Clay.

His brother James, following the usual custom of the times, resided over the bank, first in Paradise Street, and then in Lord Street. When, on 15th October 1799, he married Miss Rigg, he quitted these bachelor rooms, and took up his residence at 1 Duke Street.

Thomas Parke, another of the partners, was a descendant of a family long resident in Liverpool. His grandfather was a successful captain in the West India trade. He had two sons, Thomas, who was in business in Liverpool as an ironmonger and anchorsmith, and John, who was a merchant in Abchurch Lane, London. Whether these two brothers had ventures in common is

---

[1] George Case was son of John Case of Prescot. He became a successful Liverpool merchant, and was Mayor in 1781. When John Gregson died in 1807, George Case succeeded him as Receiver-General of Taxes for the County of Lancaster. He died 2nd November 1836, aged 88, at his residence, Walton Priory.

not known, but they both figured in the same *Gazette*, 22nd November 1758. Their mother Dorothy, then a widow, was so affected by these misfortunes that she immediately took to her bed, and died broken-hearted early in December. She lived in the present Derby Square, and her household goods were sold by auction in January 1759.

It will give some indication of the widespread interest taken in privateering when it is remarked that the managers of and principal shareholders in a (then) large vessel of 250 tons, 16 carriage guns, 20 swivels, and 154 men, were Thomas Parke, ironmonger, and Stanhope Mason, draper.

Thomas Parke, subsequently banker, was son of this Thomas Parke, and appears in our earliest directory, 1766, as Thomas Parke & Co., linen merchants, Covent Garden. By 1769 they had removed to Old Church Yard, and later on their business was transferred to Chorley Street. He, in common with the other Liverpool merchants, at first lived over his business premises, but by 1784 he had a house in the fashionable Duke Street. He had by the regular process of evolution risen from trader to shipowner and privateer owner. Matters prospered, and about 1781 he had bought and occupied Highfield House, West Derby. This spacious mansion was formerly the residence

of the Dowager-Duchess of Atholl,[1] and had
about 34 acres of grounds attached. He, in
the course of time, acquired additional lands,
so that when the property was offered for sale
in 1828, after the death of his widow, the surrounding estate amounted to 120 acres. It was
lavishly kept up, and extensive hot-houses were
erected.

Though a wealthy man, Thomas Parke took
no active interest in municipal affairs.

He and his wife Anne, daughter of William
Preston, had several children.

The eldest son was Thomas John Parke, equally
well known in his day as Thomas Parke, jun.
He entered the banking firm, and will occupy
our attention hereafter. He married, 22nd
October 1804, the daughter of John Colquitt,
Town Clerk of Liverpool.

The second son was Preston Fryers Parke,
afterwards Major of 1st Regiment of Duke of

---

[1] The Isle of Man had been sold by the 3rd Duke of Atholl in
1765, but he and his descendants retained the right of appointing the
Bishop and many of the clergy. The residence at Highfield proved
an excellent thing for the Liverpool clergy, several of whom received
the bishopric. Of one presentation Smithers ("Liverpool") tells a
capital story. Rev. Claudius Crigan was minister of St. Anne's, and
being in a very uncertain state of health, when Dr. Mason died in
1784 he was appointed bishop by the Duchess of Atholl, who thought
that the See would again become vacant by the time her son, who was
then a minor, would be ready to take possession; but contrary to
expectation, he lived to possess the bishopric twenty-five years. The
son of the Duchess died in the interim.

Lancaster's Own Militia. He died *s.p.*, 2nd
February 1832, at Ceynsham Bank, Cheltenham.

Two other sons were John and Ralph, who
both died *s.p.*

The youngest son was James, first of the
Middle Temple, barrister-at-law, next Baron
Parke, and subsequently Lord Wensleydale.

Born 22nd March 1782, he married, 8th April
1817, Cecilia Arabella Frances Barlow, youngest
daughter of Samuel Barlow of Middlethorp, near
York. Having no surviving male successor, Sir
James Parke was deemed by Lord Palmerston in
1856 a proper person on whom to confer a
life peerage. But the House of Lords would
have none of it, and the outcome was that the
usual patent had to be substituted for the proposed one. His title was Baron Wensleydale of
Walton, in the county of Lancaster. His eldest
daughter, Cecilia Anne, married, 21st September
1841, Sir Matthew White Ridley, 4th Baronet,
and her son was the first Viscount Ridley, who
died 28th November 1904. She died 20th
April 1845. Lord Wensleydale died 25th February 1868, in the eighty-sixth year of his age.[1]

---

[1] Two brief notices of Baron Parke by a good judge may be given:
" Baron Parke was a great lawyer, and educated for the law, when the
cultivation of advocacy and great knowledge of the law were essential
to success."

" Baron Parke was one of the shrewdest of men, as any one would
discover who attempted to deceive him."—" Reminiscences of Sir
Henry Hawkins," 1904.

During his lifetime his fondness of legal subtleties gained for him a suggested epitaph :—

Hic jacet Jacobus Parke,
Qui leges Angliæ in absurdum reduxit.

Thomas Parke had also three daughters. The eldest, Hannah, was unmarried, and died 25th March 1827.

The second, Alice, was married, 1st August 1791, at Walton, Liverpool, to Sitwell Sitwell, son of Francis Sitwell of Renishaw, Derbyshire. They had two daughters and a son. The latter, George, was born 20th April 1797, and his mother died the following month. Sitwell Sitwell was created a baronet on 3rd October 1808.

The third, Ann, was married, 23rd September 1805, to John Groome Smythe of Worsfield, Shropshire, and died his widow, 4th November 1852.

The remaining partner in the firm was Thomas Morland. He had been in the employ of William Gregson for many years, and had acted as liquidator of the various firms in which William Gregson had been interested, and which in process of time had been dissolved. He in 1781 was resident in Hanover Street, married on 26th July 1789 Alice, daughter of Robert Williamson, and by 1790 resided

in Seel Street.   He came from a Knutsford
family.

William Gregson, alike from his business con-
nections as from his municipal position, had great
influence in the town, and it is not surprising
to find that the Corporation accounts, yearly
rapidly increasing in value, were kept with
Gregson & Co.

The firm commenced its business in Paradise
Street, but soon it gravitated nearer to the centre
of commerce, the Exchange.

Early in 1792 it occupied premises at No. 13
Lord Street.   It will be convenient here to call
to remembrance that Lord Street was not the
broad spacious street we now have.   On the contrary, it was a narrow, confined street.   Castle
Street then ran in an unbroken line across the
present splendid mouth of Lord Street right to
Cable Street, and the entrances from Castle Street
were through Castle Ditch, on the north side
from Harrington Street, on the south from Cable
Street.

Here Gregson & Co. were when the panic of
1793 took possession of England.   They suffered,
and on April 15, 1793, they issued the following
notice : " The creditors of William Gregson,
Sons, Parke, & Morland are requested to meet at
the bank on Wednesday next, at ten o'clock, to
receive the report of Messrs. Walker, Case, and

Leyland,[1] who have undertaken to inspect their affairs, and to adopt such measures as shall be sufficiently expedient for the general interest of every person concerned."

Gregsons survived this ordeal, but reconstructed the firm. Their circular, dated 25th November 1793, is as follows: "The banking business heretofore carried on by Messrs. William Gregson, Sons, Parke, & Morland will in future be transacted under the firm of William Gregson, Sons, Parkes, & Clay." [2]

Thomas Morland left the firm, and we find him in 1796 living at 3 Slater Street, described as "gentleman." In the directory for 1800 no entry is made of the name.[3]

[1] They were three of the principal merchants of the town. Richard Walker was the son of Richard Walker, merchant, who in November 1759 had married the sister of Richard Watt, merchant in Kingston, Jamaica. The latter amassed a large fortune, came home on 11th August 1782, died in 1796, aged 72, leaving half a million sterling between his two nephews, Richard Watt and Richard Walker. The latter married on 11th December 1787 the eldest daughter of Edward Wilson, but she died 23rd October 1788, in her twenty-first year. He then married on 1st June 1790 the daughter of William James. He died 1801.

For George Case, see *ante*, p. 111; and for Thomas Leyland, see Leyland and Bullins, p. 169.

[2] Richard Brooke ("Ancient Liverpool," p. 254) puts the date of this change at 1795 or 1796; but evidently he was not aware of this circular.

[3] In the directory of 1803 there is a Thomas Morland, coast waiter, Rodney Street. About 1811 he removed to Brownlow Street, where he died, 2nd February 1819, aged 65. Whether or not these two are identical, I have been unable to ascertain. The ages would appear to be about the same in both cases, and both came from Knutsford.

The new partners were Thomas John Parke
and Henry Clay.   The first was the son of
Thomas Parke, and had been with the bank for
some years.   Both he and Henry Clay had been
appointed members of the Town Council on 7th
November 1792.   He graduated to bailiff in
1794.   At this time he was joint-tenant with
James Gregson of the bank house in Lord
Street, but on his marriage, 20th October
1804, to the daughter of John Colquitt, the
Town Clerk, he took a house in Ranelagh
Place.

Henry Clay was the son of Richard Clay, who
died 28th October 1774.   The latter was an
eminent tobacco manufacturer, residing in Church
Street, with his warehouses and manufactory in
School Lane.   The title of his firm was Clay &
Midgley.   When in 1774 his son succeeded him,
the title of the firm became Clay, Holding, &
Parry, and so continued till 1790, when the style
became Clay, Parry, & Midgley.   Henry Clay
continued to live with his widowed mother[1] at
23 Church Street, till on his marriage, 25th
April 1791, with Miss Frances Wilson, he removed to 62 Duke Street.

As stated above, he was appointed to the Town
Council 7th November 1792.   He became bailiff
in 1793, the year in which he joined the bank.

[1] Mrs. Clay died 4th September 1794.

His sister had married his partner, John Gregson, in 1786. The firm thus reconstituted progressed favourably, and by 1796 John Gregson had obtained the office, with large emoluments, of Receiver-General of the Land Tax for the county of Lancaster, and had removed his abode to 6 Slater Street. But the senior, William Gregson, died on the 28th December 1800, aged 81, being then father of the Corporation of Liverpool. John Gregson thereupon removed to the mansion at Everton, and here in 1803 he entertained Prince William of Gloucester.

In 1805 Henry Clay became Mayor. But trouble was in store for the bank. On 25th November 1805 the following circular was issued :—

" The co-partnership carried on by us under the name of Gregsons, Parkes, & Clay, as bankers, is this day dissolved by mutual consent.

(Signed)   JNO. GREGSON.
            JAS. GREGSON.
            THOS. PARKE.
            THOS. J. PARKE.
            HENRY CLAY."

The business was continued by John Gregson, James Gregson, and Henry Clay.

Some undisclosed scandalous conduct in the bank's affairs on the part of Thomas J. Parke was the reason for the dissolution. But there can be no doubt that the defection of the Parkes caused a considerable weakening of the bank's capital.

The new partnership continued business till 21st April 1807, when John Gregson committed suicide by hanging himself at his house in Everton, being then aged 52.

The bank then ceased business, and its affairs dragged on for a great number of years. Smithers ("Liverpool," p. 167. Liverpool, 1825) says that upon the final adjustment of the concerns, recently made, the full amount of all the debts were paid.

In January 1808 the freehold and other properties belonging to the bank were offered for sale. Among them was a moiety of the "Golden Lion Inn," Dale Street, which in 1837–8 became the site of the building of the Liverpool Royal Bank.

Early in April 1807 the Corporation of Liverpool voted Henry Clay a piece of plate valued at 100 guineas, as a testimony of the Corporation to the respectful attention shown to H.R.H. the Prince of Wales on his visit to Liverpool.

He had recently taken a country house in Lodge Lane, and at this he lived in retirement for some years.

But the Corporation of Liverpool, whatever its faults, did not forget its friends. On 17th June

1811 James Gildart, Receiver of the Dock Duties, died *suddenly*, and the *very next day* the Corporation appointed Henry Clay to the vacant office.   Later on he resided at 15 Wavertree Road, where he died suddenly on 28th May 1828. He is described by "The Old Stager" as a "frank, jovial, light-hearted fellow."

But if the Corporation could thus reward one of its members, it could also punish others. Under date 5th December 1813 the Council minutes run :—

"The opinions of Mr. Holroyd and Mr. Scarlett, relative to the power of this Council to remove Mr. Thomas John Parke, one of the members, for his gross misconduct when a partner in the late banking house of Messrs. Gregson & Co., and for his continued neglect of attendance at the Council of this Borough, having been read,

"Resolved and ordered, that the regular summons requiring the attendance of Mr. Parke at the next Council be served upon him and repeated, as recommended in the Opinions, with a view to the expulsion of Mr. Parke as one of the members of the Council."

"1814, *April 6th.*—Resolved that the resignation of Mr. Thomas John Parke as one of the members of the Council signified in his letter to the Mayor—now read— be and the same is hereby accepted."

It is curious to note that although Mr. T. J. Parke is thus stated in the Council minutes to have been allowed to resign, yet at the Com-

mission held in 1833 to inquire into the Liverpool Corporation, Mr. John Foster, the then
Town Clerk, stated that the Corporation possessed
power to expel its members, which they had exercised in two instances, Mr. Thomas John Parke
and Mr. Weston.

After a while Mr. T. J. Parke retired to
France, becoming one of the large army of
refugees, who, leaving their country for their
country's good, yet drew considerable sums
from their estates, without contributing to the
heavy taxation of the period. He died at
his residence, Beau Séjour, near Tours, on 5th
September 1823.

His father, Thomas Parke, continued his residence at Highfield, "a fine, glorious, jovial old
man," in the words of "The Old Stager," until
his death, 30th November 1819, aged 90. His
wife, Anne, survived him till 16th December
1827, being then in her eighty-eighth year.

The remaining partner, James Gregson, continued his independent business, and by 1811 had
removed from Great George Street to 46 Rodney
Street, then having an insurance office at the
north side of the Town Hall. Both the private
and business addresses indicate a certain amount
of well-being, but later traces of him are not
available.

His character is preserved by " The Old

Stager," whose thumb-nail sketches are all of
men he had met. " We had also our circle of
wits. . . . Jim Gregson, who lived in Rodney
Street, a man of racy humour, with a fund of
originality about him which revelled in the utter-
ance of good things."

CHAPTER IX

THOMAS, SAMUEL, AND JOSEPH CRANE.

THIS was by no means an important firm, and had, as *a bank*, but a short existence. The first of the family who honoured Liverpool with his presence was Samuel, who having had some London experience in book-selling, commenced business on 24th November 1775 at 43 Water Street, opposite the Talbot Hotel, as a bookseller and stationer. Early in July 1777 he was married at St. Anne's Church to Miss Glass. His brothers, Thomas and Joseph, were grocers in Chester, having a dwelling-house and land at Boughton, where they carried on the manufacture of stone and Prussian blue. The three joined hands, and on 16th November 1786 the following circular appeared : " Thomas, Samuel, and Joseph Crane respectfully inform the public that they have opened a bank, the corner of Dale Street, near the Exchange, where business in that line will be regularly transacted on liberal terms." This house was numbered 174 Dale Street. In

October 1787 they had a fire on their premises, which did but little damage. As illustrative of the time is added the newspaper remark : " They were insured—a pleasing precaution." In December of the same year Joseph Crane removed his bookselling and stationery business (which included patent medicines, &c.) to the corner of Mathew Street and John Street. On 10th June 1788 a commission in bankruptcy was issued against them, and by December of that year a dividend of 6s. 8d. in the £ had been paid on debts " to which there was no objection." Those debts to which there was objection included bills issued by them " payable to fictitious payees," so that the class of business done by Cranes may readily be inferred.

It appears that the house in John Street was their property, and this, with a house on the west side of Hope Street, with garden attached, were sold by auction. The Chester properties too came under the hammer.

Other dividends were paid in 1792, 1794, and 1796.

Castle Street was widened in 1786, and in that and the following year the west side was rebuilt. In February 1789 Samuel Crane notifies the public " that he has removed to the new side of Castle Street, four doors from the corner of Brunswick Street, nearer the Exchange." This was numbered 58 in 1790. By the directory of 1796 the business appears as Crane & Jones, and this firm published *The Liverpool Guide*. By 1800 the name of Crane had disappeared.

CHAPTER X

Staniforth, Ingram, Bold, & Daltera—The partners, and their con-
nections—Ingram, Kennett & Ingram of Wakefield—Dissolution
of partnership.

THE banking firm under the above style had not
a long career, but the several partners were fully
typical of their time. Full of energy and resource, they engaged in multifarious businesses,
and enjoyed considerable reputation in their day
and generation.

They commenced business as bankers at the
latter end of 1791, and closed on the 1st January
1795. The banking house was in Pool Lane
(now South Castle Street), at the corner of
Litherland Alley, immediately opposite King
Street. The partners were Thomas Staniforth,
Francis Ingram, Jonas Bold, and Joseph Daltera.

THOMAS STANIFORTH was an eminent merchant, principally engaged in the Greenland
fisheries. This business was commenced in
Liverpool in 1750 by Charles Goore, Bailiff in
1747, Mayor in 1754–5 and 1767, who died

13th March 1783, aged 81. His wife Margery,
daughter of Henry Halsall of Everton, died
12th August 1776, aged 70. About 1764 (?)
Thomas Staniforth appears to have married their
daughter Elizabeth, and on Charles Goore's retirement from business some time prior to 1774
(his son Henry having died 7th August 1771,
aged 35), Thomas Staniforth joined the business
of himself and his father-in-law. Goore had
also a ropery extending from Ranelagh Street to
the south end of Renshaw Street, and to this
Thomas Staniforth also succeeded. When Ranelagh Street was built up and Lawton Street
formed, the offices of and entrance to the rope-
walks were in the latter street. A large business
was done in supplying cordage, &c., to the rapidly
increasing number of mercantile and privateer
vessels.

The products of the Greenland fisheries were
seal skins, seal oil, whalebone and whale oil,
Staniforth's warehouse for the whalebone being
at the top of Hanover Street.

Thomas Staniforth is given in our earliest
directories as residing in Union Street, but by 1777
he had built and occupied a large mansion in
Ranelagh Street. This eventually became the
famous Lynn's "Waterloo Hotel," and its site
is now occupied by the Central Station. He was
also a partner in a wine, rum, and brandy firm,

THOMAS STANIFORTH

but this was dissolved 1st July 1776, the business being continued by his partners, Richard Machell and Thomas Burton. Like the vast majority of the merchants of Liverpool, he had shares in slavers, and on the formation of the African Association in July 1777 he was appointed a member of the first committee. As early as 1774 he was elected to the Chamber of Commerce, and continued his services for many years.

He took an active part in municipal government, having been appointed to the Town Council in 1781, in which year he also became Bailiff. He was elected Mayor in 1797, after an extremely severe contest. He was a man of enlightened views, and was in 1789, on the founding of the Liverpool Marine Society for the benefit of masters of vessels, their widows and children, appointed first President. He was interested in music, and was at one time President of the Music Hall, the forerunner of our present Philharmonic Society. He died 15th December 1803, in his sixty-ninth year, his wife surviving him till 29th January 1822, being then aged 84. They had a daughter, who died 13th February 1791, aged 26.

The son, Samuel Staniforth, who succeeded to the business and residence, was a notable character. He is frequently referred to in the election squibs as "Surly" or "Sulky Sam,"

which his temperament justified, and he had the
reputation of being the ugliest man in Liverpool.
He was Bailiff in 1804, and Mayor in 1812, but
later in life he did not prosper in business, and
obtained the post of Distributor of Stamps. He
died 5th April 1851, aged 82, his wife Mary,
who was connected with the Littledales, having
predeceased him on 24th August 1846, being
then aged 73. When in business he had as a
partner in the rope-making concern William
Laird, but the partnership was dissolved 31st
December 1821.[1]

Samuel's son was Thomas, who entered the
Church, and was in 1832 inducted to the rectory
of Bolton-in-Bowland, on the presentation of
John Bolton of Storrs, Windermere.[2]

1 William Laird then went to Birkenhead, and joined Daniel Horton
as boiler-makers. This partnership was dissolved 4th October 1828,
William Laird continuing.

2 John Bolton was the retired wealthy West Indian merchant and
active Liverpool politician, whose house in Duke Street witnessed
many notable election events. He was a vigorous supporter of
Canning, and from the balcony of his house Canning made his last
public speech in Liverpool. On the resumption of the war with
France in 1803 Bolton raised and equipped at his sole expense a
regiment of 800 men. This, the 1st Battalion of the Liverpool
Volunteers, he commanded, and he is therefore constantly referred to
as Colonel Bolton. He had willed his country seat, Storrs, Windermere, with 3000 acres of land surrounding it, to Harold Littledale, but,
in consequence of the latter having lost £3000 in helping a Scotch-
man to work a kelp invention in the Western Isles, he altered his will
and devised the estate to the Staniforth family, the Rev. Thomas
Staniforth succeeding, with a proviso that failing male heirs it should
revert to Harold Littledale. The Rev. Thomas Staniforth died in

FRANCIS INGRAM, the second partner, was an
excellent sample of the old Liverpool merchant,
shrewd, capable, courageous. The business in
Liverpool was commenced by his brother
William, who had his office and residence at
the house in Pool Lane, where the bank we
are now considering subsequently made its home.
They were sons of William Ingram of Oulton,
near Wakefield, and of Sarah, daughter of Elizabeth Bradley. The latter was daughter of John
Bever, through whom the Ingrams inherited a
considerable amount of property in Wakefield,
including that even now remarkable timbered
house known as the "Six Chimneys," in Kirkgate. William Ingram died 27th June 1753, at
the early age of 49, and his widow, Sarah, survived
him till 8th December 1780, being then aged 75.

William the younger was early to the fore in
business, and in respect in the town.

When Thurot was ravaging the British coasts,
the Liverpool Corporation and the inhabitants

1886, and under the proviso the estate passed to Harold Littledale's
only daughter, Sarah Annabella, who had married, 25th August 1874,
Sir Thomas Fletcher Boughey, Bart., of Aqualate, co. Stafford.
The Rev. Thomas Staniforth rowed in the first race between Oxford
and Cambridge, and dined with the crews on the fiftieth anniversary
of that race. Samuel Staniforth had an only daughter, Sarah, who
married, 31st May 1828, Frederick Greenwood of Swarcliffe Hall,
Yorks. They had a son, John, whose third son, Edwin Wilfred, succeeded to the Rev. Thomas Staniforth's property, and on 7th December
1887 assumed by Royal Licence the name and arms of Stanyforth. He
is of Kirk Hammerton Hall, Yorks.

successfully raised four companies of volunteers
for the defence of the town.   Each company
was accoutred at its own expense.   One of the
companies was captained by William Ingram,
and made a brave show on review in 1760 "in
scarlet coats and breeches, lapelled and faced with
green, green waistcoats, gold-laced hats, and
queue wigs."   He was then but twenty-four
years of age.   He was a good sportsman, had
his game-cock matches, and raced his horses
against rivals for 100 guineas a side.

When Sir William Meredith contested Liverpool in 1761, one of his principal supporters,
and host during the election, was William
Ingram.   On the declaration of the poll, Sir
William was chaired from the Exchange to the
house in Pool Lane.

About 1767 William Ingram retired to Oulton,
near Wakefield, and died 14th October 1770,
aged 34.   He by will, dated 31st January 1763,
devised his estate to his mother Sarah.

His brother John had died November 1758,
aged 21.   He had properties in Kirkgate, Wakefield, contiguous to the "Six Chimneys," which
had been surrendered to him in 1750 by John
Bever, and in 1766 his property was conveyed
to his "only surviving brother and next heir,
Francis."   This does not agree with the fact
that William was then living.

Sarah Ingram, by will dated 27th March 1776, appointed her estate to her son Francis, who thus practically came into all the family property.

He succeeded to his brother's business and premises in Liverpool about 1767. The business was that of a general merchant. Needless to say that it included the "African" or slave trade. We find him in 1772 dealing in ivory, teeth, and hardwoods, and he became a member of the first African Committee in 1777.

Francis Ingram & Co. also were interested in privateers during the War of Independence and the subsequent war with France. Fortunately some records of this house survive, and some of the letters of instruction given by them to Captain Haslam of the *Enterprise* privateer are given *in extenso* in Gomer Williams' "The Liverpool Privateers." They show great administrative ability, and are happy examples of the care, forethought, and capacity displayed by a Liverpool merchant of this date. Partners in their enterprise were Thomas and William Earle and Thomas Leyland. Francis Ingram had also a share in a ropery business, under the title of Ingram, Brown, & Co., but this was dissolved in March 1778, and the business continued by Thomas Brown. Towards 1789 he advertised his house for sale, as he was preparing to quit

Liverpool for Wakefield, to which he was drawn by so many family ties. It did not find a purchaser, and he appears as occupier in the directory of 1790, possibly continuing in possession until it was taken over by the bank in 1791.

In Wakefield he started a banking firm, Ingram, Kennett, & Ingram, his partners being his son, Abraham Richard Ingram, and Benjamin Kennett. He also opened a similar business at Halifax, his partners being his three sons, William, Henry, and Abraham Richard, and one Robert Witham. Precisely when these businesses were started is not known, but we find that, on 7th November 1792, a marriage took place at Eccles between Benjamin Kennett of Wakefield, *banker*, and Miss Cath. Steer of the same place.

Some of Francis Ingram's businesses in Liverpool were continued. He had acquired the works on Copperas Hill for the manufacture of copperas, and under the style of Ingram and Spranger the manufacture was there continued until June 1807, when the works were transferred to Litherland.[1]

Other interests were continued under the title of Ingrams, Rigby, & Co., which firm had offices

[1] Picton ("Memorials of Liverpool," vol. ii. 202, ed. 1875) says the copperas works on Copperas Hill were discontinued before 1796. This is incorrect: they were discontinued in the name of the former proprietor, Richard Hughes. In the map of 1796, as Picton notes, the works are still shown.

first in Lower Castle Street, and later in Heywood's Yard, Gradwell Street.   The partnership
was continued until 31st October 1803, the
public notice of dissolution being issued so late
as 8th April 1805.   The then partners were
Francis Ingram of Wakefield, banker, William
Ingram of Halifax, banker, James Rigby of West
Derby Breck, merchant, and Richard Butler of
9 Kent Square, merchant.

In the directory for 1807 the style of the firm
is given as Ingrams & Butler, merchants, 19 Parr
Street.   Hence it would appear that the dissolution of partnership was only as regards James
Rigby.   The firm is given as shipowners in the
list of Bidston signals for 1808.

In 1807 the bank at Wakefield became involved, the then partners being Francis Ingram,
Benjamin Kennett Dawson, and Abraham Richard
Ingram.   They executed a deed, 9th July 1807,
to certain trustees, making the real and personal
property of each of the partners liable for the
debts due by the bank.   Further, on 19th and
20th October 1809 other deeds were executed by
Francis Ingram, making over his estates in Wakefield to the same trustees, subject to a debt due
by the bank to their London agents, Messrs.
Williams & Co.   For the security of that debt
Francis Ingram had deposited with Messrs.
Williams & Co. the title-deeds of the estate.

The co-partnership at Halifax was found indebted
to the co-partnership at Wakefield, and the property was conveyed so that the proceeds of sale
should be applied in discharge of the debt of
the Halifax house to the Wakefield one.   It
is satisfactory to note that at the finish all the
debts of the bank were paid in full.

Francis Ingram continued to reside in St.
John's Place, Wakefield, where he died, 28th
August 1815, aged 76.   His wife, Christian,
survived him till 17th February 1816, being
then aged 74.

They were both buried beneath the chancel of
All Saints, the parish church of Wakefield, now
the Cathedral Church.   Here also were buried
the parents of Francis, William, and Sarah, with
their other children, William, John, and Eliza.

Also Catherine, Ann, Sarah, Mary, and Henry,
children of Francis and Christian Ingram;
Henry was the youngest son, and died 13th
March 1850, aged 69.

Also Frances, who died 15th September 1831,
aged 65, the wife of John, the son of Francis,
also their children, Thomas, Frederick, and
Caroline.

The stones which recorded the above were
covered over when the chancel was paved with
tiles, but brasses were placed on the spots corresponding to the burying-places.

In 1866, by the will of Abraham Richard
Ingram, a monument to the memory of his
parents was raised in the church by the filling
·of the east window with new tracery and painted
glass at a cost of £800. On a brass below the
window is the following inscription :—

"In memoriam Francisci et Christianæ Ingram
Parentum hanc fenestram vitream ex testamento
Abrahæ Ricardi filii eorum heredes reficiendum et
pictura ornandum curaverunt a.d. mdccclxvi."

It is not found that Francis Ingram's eldest
son, John, was ever identified with any of the
businesses. He married, 11th February 1794,
at Wycliffe, Yorks, Frances, only daughter and
heiress of William Gream of Heath, near Halifax.
In 1833 he erected a brass at the west end of the
south aisle of Wakefield Church to the memory
of his parents, Francis and Christian, his daughter
Caroline, and his wife Frances. His son, Hugh
Francis, placed a memorial brass at the west end
of the north aisle to his father and sister. After
stating that John died 30th January 1841, and
giving like particulars of the sister, it says:—

"Deo scilicet animas reddiderunt. Romæ
Urbis intra muros sepulchrum habent."

From the fact that in all these inscriptions no
mention is made of Francis's son William, one
of his former partners at Halifax, the author

is inclined to connect with this family the following, who carried on business as coal merchants in Oldhall Street, and were interred in St. Philip's, Hardman Street, Liverpool:—

William Ingram, *d.* 16 Oct. 1824, aged 56.
Jane, wife of do., *d.* 29 Nov. 1819, aged 46.
Francis Ingram, *d.* 16 Jan. 1825, aged 50.

Both the names and the ages point to this inclusion.

The third partner, JONAS BOLD, was a member of a very old Liverpool family. He commenced business on his own account early, having acquired in 1768 "The Old Sugar Mold Works," near the Folly (now Islington), formerly carried on in the name of Charles Wood & Co. He was then in his twenty-third year. "At the works were made sugar moulds and drips, chimney moulds, large jars for water, black mugs of sizes, crucibles and melting pots for silversmiths, founders," &c. But, of course, he must needs go in for the African trade. In 1777 he was one of the African merchants who formed a committee to regulate this business. His firm during the wars with America, France, Spain, and Holland despatched their privateers, in common with the majority of Liverpool merchants. In the early part of his career he lived at 64 Strand Street. Not far off, at 14 Redcross Street, near the

corner of Strand Street, lived Isaac Oldham,
sugar merchant. The writer is unable to trace
any relationship between the two, but on the
death of the latter on 14th July 1782, aged 76,
Jonas Bold succeeded to the mansion and the
business. Bold's third son was born in 1785, and
was christened Isaac Oldham. Redcross Street
at this time was a very fashionable street. Here
Jonas Bold lived in luxury for many years. He
was chosen by the Common Council to be one
of their body, became Bailiff in 1796, and Mayor
in 1802, after a contest. He belonged to the
Conservative party, yet in 1790, when a memorial
was addressed to the Mayor and Bailiffs, signify-
ing strong dissent from the manner of selecting
members for the Council, and objecting to some
members who had been chosen, we find his name
as one of the signatories. The matter complained
of was not remedied until after the Parliamentary
Enquiry into the Corporation in 1833.

In 1797, when news reached Liverpool of the
invasion of England at Fishguard by the French,
the usual active spirit was displayed. One
thousand volunteers were immediately enrolled,
and were divided into eight companies. Of one
of these Jonas Bold was captain. His house was
on the south side of Redcross Street, below Sea
Brow, and he transferred all the sugar business
of Isaac Oldham to his own premises in Strand

Street, from which he constructed a counting-house and sugar warehouses, jointly known as Bold's Court.

Sometime prior to 1807 he acquired a house in Burlington Street, Bath, where he died, 20th October 1822, aged 77.

His eldest son, Arthur, became Vicar of Stoke Pogis, Bucks, and died there, 21st January 1831. The second son, Peter, died in Jersey, 5th August 1832. The third son, Isaac Oldham, married, 18th June 1816, Elizabeth, daughter of the late John Gregson of Everton (see Gregson & Co.). He was a merchant, entered the Town Council, and became Bailiff in 1827, at the same time as Samuel Thompson, one of the partners in Heywood's Bank. He died 5th December 1853, aged 68, and his wife Elizabeth died 26th May 1857, aged 61.

Bold Street is named after Jonas Bold, who in 1786 had a lease of the land granted him by the Corporation. He forthwith proceeded to lay out the street. He also owned land at the top of the street, extending over the site of St. Luke's Church. He also owned by 1790 several acres of land in Everton, near St. Domingo Mere.

The remaining partner was JOSEPH DALTERA, also a merchant. One of his early advertisements has caused certain ill-informed people to imagine that the sale of human beings was the regular

custom in Liverpool. This, of course, was not
the case. The fact that practically the whole of
the sales took place far beyond the ken of the
man in the street was one of the main causes of
the apathetic attitude of the bulk of the people
towards the viciousness of the slave trade. Had
the horrors of the traffic been before their eyes,
there is no doubt but that the iniquity would have
been swept away long before the time when, by
the persistent efforts of noble philanthropists, this
was accomplished. The instances of actual sale
might be counted on the fingers of one hand,
though it is notorious that a black attendant,
regarded certainly as a chattel, was the frequent
apanage of a fashionable establishment.

The advertisement, appearing under date 17th
June 1757, is as follows :—

"To be sold 10 pipes of raisin wine, a parcel of
bottled cyder, and a negro boy, apply to Joseph Daltera,
merchant, in Union Street, who sells at his warehouse
near the Salt House, Dock Gates, fine, second, and coarse
flour."

He prospered for a while in business, and in
1774 we find him elected to the Chamber of
Commerce. But in 1778 he was declared bankrupt, his partners being John Dobson and John
Walker, deceased. He appears to have soon
rehabilitated himself, for in 1780 he was again

elected to the Chamber of Commerce. His life, after his becoming a partner in the bank, was but short. He had, after one or two changes of address, settled down in the fashionable Hanover Street sometime prior to 1774, and here he resided till his death, 2nd October 1793.

His wife Jane survived him thirty-three years, dying at her house in Rodney Street, 10th January 1826, in the ninetieth year of her age.

They had a son Joseph, though no one ever called him by that name : to every one he was "Joe." Nominally he was an attorney and notary, but his real life was that of a diner out. In demand as a wit and *raconteur*, he wasted his undoubted talents in one long round of dining and dissipation. "The Old Stager" has many amusing pages of his sayings and doings.

As before stated, the bank existed but a few years. It is not mentioned in Gore's "Directory," because there was no issue of that valuable volume between 1790 and 1796. But in the brief period of its existence it had experience of one of the stormiest times that ever the banking and commerce of England were subjected to. The strain caused by the declaration of war with France in 1793 was well-nigh intolerable, and in Liverpool led to a remarkable and bold experiment, detailed in a separate chapter, to counteract the universal distrust.

x   DISSOLUTION OF PARTNERSHIP   143

The circular notifying the dissolution is as follows :—

"The partnership in the banking house at Liverpool, carried on under the firm of Staniforth, Ingram, Bold, and Daltera, was dissolved by mutual consent on 1st January 1795. Witness our hands :

THOMAS STANIFORTH.
FRANCIS INGRAM.
JONAS BOLD.
JAMES DALTERA.
Exor. of late Jos. DALTERA.

LIVERPOOL, *April* 14, 1795."

Fancy a modern bank giving notice of a dissolution of partnership four months after the event !

CHAPTER XI

THE LIVERPOOL CORPORATION ISSUE
OF NOTES.

The panic of 1793—Special meeting and resolutions of Town Council
—Appointment of joint-committee of Common Councilmen and
merchants—Report—Meetings of merchants and resolutions—
Application for assistance to Bank of England—Refusal of application—Application to Parliament by petition for leave to
bring in a Bill authorising the issue of negotiable notes—Statement of Corporation property—Bill passed—Issue of notes—
Early retirement of notes—All loans paid off.

WHEN the panic that set in, on the declaration of war by France in 1793, ruined many
merchants of the highest status, overthrew
Charles Caldwell & Co., and menaced the other
bankers and merchants in the town, it was felt
that a united effort was needed to cope with the
situation. The then Mayor, Clayton Tarleton,
on the 20th March 1793 held a meeting of the
principal merchants of Liverpool in the Exchange. Sundry resolutions were passed, and
in compliance with one of them the Mayor
called a special meeting of the Council, which
was held the same day. The report of this

meeting, taken from the Corporation Records, is as follows :—

> "1793, *March* 20.
> "CLAYTON TARLETON, *Mayor.*

"The Mayor having reported to this Council that the late extensive failures, particularly of some great commercial and banking houses in London, were almost immediately followed with the failure of a very old and principal banking house in Liverpool ; that the latter failure had now caused such an alarm in this town and its neighbourhood, that not only the other banking houses were greatly distressed, but there was an apprehension of a general calamity to the merchants, traders, and inhabitants of this place, and to the County of Lancaster at large, from the shock to public confidence and from the want of immediate pecuniary resource. That under this impression he had this day held a meeting of some of the principal merchants in the Exchange, at which several resolutions were entered into, and they had unanimously subscribed the following paper, earnestly requesting him to convene the Common Council to consider whether it might not be proper to offer the Corporate Seal to the Bank of England for a loan of money to assist the credit of this place by an application under the direction of a Committee, composed of an equal number of Members of the Common Council and of respectable Merchants out of the Council, or to consider whether it was possible for the Common Council, by taking measures in their Corporate capacity, to avert the common ruin that seemed to threaten the commerce of the town.

"It is, therefore, now unanimously resolved by the

K

Council that the very unprecedented and truly alarming state of the public credit of this country, and of this town in particular, does, in the opinion of this Council, well justify the Meeting of the Merchants held here this day and the requisition made for the convening of this Special Council.

"That the representations now made of the distresses of all commercial persons in this town do well deserve the very serious attention of this Council, so as to induce them to consider whether any, and what, effectual relief can be afforded in their Corporate capacity. That they, therefore, do now nominate the following six members, viz. the Mayor, Mr. Alderman Earle, Mr. Alderman William Crosbie, junior, Mr. Alderman Case, Mr. Brooks, and Mr. Statham, a Committee to confer with the same number of gentlemen appointed by the Merchants at large at their meeting held this day in the Exchange; that such Committee be requested to prepare themselves with a report of what they may consider proper to be done; the same to be made at a further Special Council which the Mayor is now instructed to call to be held to-morrow evening at six o'clock."

The members appointed at the meeting of merchants to the joint-committee were Messrs. John Brown, Edward Falkner, Richard Walker, Thomas Hayhurst, Thomas Leyland, and Jacob Nelson.

The committee met and prepared a report, which was presented to the Council at their special meeting on 21st March. The report reads :—

"That they had found, after an interview with the four existing banking houses in the town, that the sum of a hundred thousand pounds was wanted, and would be sufficient to answer the present exigencies ; . . . that it was expedient for the preservation of public credit that some speedy method should be adopted of raising the money ; . . . that the most desirable mode would be by an application from the Corporation to the Directors of the Bank of England through the medium of Mr. Pitt, the Chancellor of the Exchequer, and of the Lords of the Treasury ; . . . that such loan when obtained should be advanced, under the direction of the Committee through the local bankers, on satisfactory securities, within the space of fifteen months, beyond which period it was their opinion no further advances would be required."

Public notice was given by the meeting of the merchants on 20th March in the following terms :—

" We whose names are hereunto subscribed do mutually pledge ourselves to each other, and the public, that we are ready and willing to receive in payment the bills of the several Banking Houses in this town of WILLIAM CLARKE & SONS, ARTHUR HEYWOOD, SONS, & CO., WILLIAM GREGSON, SONS, PARKE, & MORLAND, and STANIFORTH, INGRAM, BOLD, & DALTERA, at ONE or

Two months' date, as hath been the usual and customary practice."

Signed by 223 merchants and firms.

On 25th March a further advertisement appeared :—

"At a GENERAL MEETING of the Merchants and Traders in this town, held in the Exchange on Wednes- the 20th inst., and at a SPECIAL COUNCIL held in the evening of the same day, to consider of the most prob- able means for restoring the public confidence in the present Stagnation of Credit, the following gentlemen were appointed a joint COMMITTEE to deliberate upon the most speedy and effectual means of accomplishing so desirable an object, viz. :—

Committee of Merchants.	Committee of Council.
John Brown,	Clayton Tarleton (Mayor),
Edward Falkner,	Alderman Earle,
Richard Walker,	Alderman Wm. Crosbie,
Thomas Hayhurst,	Jun.,
Thomas Leyland,	Alderman Case,
Jacob Nelson,	Joseph Brooks,
	Richard Statham,

which *Committee*, having sat the two following days are happy in finding that the result of their deliberations appears to have met with general approbation, and the more so as they entertain the pleasing hope of the good consequences being soon experienced : from those motives they are induced to submit the following resolution to the consideration of the public :—

" *Resolved unanimously*, That this Committee having the interest and welfare of the town of *Liverpool* very much at heart, and taking into consideration the difficulties that may arise in providing for the bills which may be returned in the present critical state of credit, DO MOST EARNESTLY RECOMMEND to the holders of such bills, as one very important means of obtaining the above laudable purpose, to make the payments as easy to the parties who may be called upon as shall be consistent with prudence to themselves : And, as in many cases, *Forbearance* may be a wise measure for the interest of the public in general, and of the bill holders in particular, this *Committee* recommend as much indulgence as the exigency of the times and their own discretion will admit, and as may be most prudent and eligible, in every point of view.

" JOHN BROWN, Chairman."

The Town Council confirmed the report of the joint-committee, and appointed a deputation to proceed to London to wait on the Chancellor of the Exchequer and the Bank of England. The application was not successful.

While negotiations were proceeding, a letter signed " A Tradesman " appeared in Williamson's *Advertiser* of 8th April recommending the pledging of the Corporation credit for three months by the issuing of notes to the amount of £100,000, £200,000, or £300,000, and referring to the Corporation of Dublin, who, it is alleged, borrow everything they want on

Debentures. This was to be in lieu of the Corporation "treating with the Bank of England for the present loan."

A special Council meeting was called for April 15.

"It having been reported by the Mayor that the negotiations with the Bank of England for the loan of £100,000 on the Bond of this Corporation not having been successful, he and the other delegates from the very urgent necessity of removing with the greatest expedition possible the present stagnation of credit in Liverpool, thought it their duty to apply, and accordingly have applied, to Parliament by petition in the names of the Mayor and others of the Common Council then in London on behalf of themselves and the rest of the Council, for leave to bring in a Bill for the purpose of empowering the Corporation to issue negotiable notes to a certain amount and for a given period, on the credit of the Estate of the said Corporation.

"This Council do fully in all respects ratify and confirm every step which has been taken, and hereby fully empower the delegates to take every measure which shall seem to them expedient and necessary in order to carry into effect the said petition."

The latter was as follows :—

"That the trade and commerce of the town have of late years greatly increased, and were continuing to do so till the stagnation of credit which has lately taken place both here and in other parts of the kingdom

checked the same, and occasioned serious alarms of
further inconvenience.

"That in the event of such a want of credit being
even for a short duration, your petitioners have great
reason to apprehend the town of Liverpool will be greatly
injured thereby, and that the manufacturers and traders
throughout the County of Lancaster will feel the effects
of it to a very great extent, by which the interest of the
public and of individuals will be materially affected and
the Estate of the Corporation of Liverpool will be much
lessened in its value.

"That this alarming evil may, your petitioners humbly
conceive, be remedied by authority being given to the
Corporation to issue negotiable notes for different sums
of money, in the whole considerably below the value of
their estates after making allowance for their present
debts, the notes to be payable with lawful interest
thereon or otherwise at a time to be limited ; provision
being made that the estate of the said Corporation shall
be subjected to the discharge of the said notes at the
period at which they shall become payable.

"With this view your petitioners are desirous of
laying before the House a precise statement of their
property and of the engagements to which it is liable
in order to enable the House to judge of the grounds of
this application."

The statement of their property is as follows.
It is to be noted that it is dated 21st March
1793, and was doubtless primarily prepared to
exhibit to the Chancellor of the Exchequer and
the Bank of England.

ℂ

GENERAL ACCOUNT AND VALUATION OF THE ESTATE
AND REVENUE BELONGING TO THE CORPORATION
OF LIVERPOOL, TAKEN THE 21ST OF MARCH 1793.

Income for 1792.

	£	s.	d.
Fines received for renewal of leases .	2270	14	4
Ground rent received for 1792 . .	1027	1	10
Rent for buildings in possession, let to tenants at will	5166	17	6
Rents for land in possession, let to tenants at will	1349	1	0
Amount of town's duties . . .	12,180	7	0
Graving docks	1701	16	5
Anchorage	211	15	3
Small tolls called ingates and outgates .	321	9	7
Weighing machine	143	4	0
Rent of seats in St. George's Church .	268	11	0
Arrears of interest from parish of Liverpool	360	0	0
	25,000	17	11

Interest and Annuities paid in 1792.

	£	s.	d.
Annual interest upon the bond debts, principally 4½ per cent. . .	15,835	14	3
Annuities upon bond	2109	12	10
Balance in favour of the Corporation [1] .	7055	10	10
	25,000	17	11

[1] In the statement given by Aikin, "Thirty Miles Around Manchester," p. 378 (London, 1795), of the Corporation Finances, there is an error of £2000 in the Revenue Statement. This has been copied into Brooke's "Ancient Liverpool," p. 408 (Liverpool, 1853).

	£	s.	d.
Value of the above articles, adding that of the land not built on, and the strand of the river . . .	1,044,776	0	0
Valuation of the debt . . .	367,816	12	0
Balance in favour of the Corporation	676,959	8	0
Exclusive of a balance due from the trustees of the docks, and of the reversionary interest of certain lots of ground laid out for building, both together estimated at . .	60,000	0	0
Exclusive also of public buildings, and ground appropriated to public purposes, valued at . .	85,000	0	0
Net value of Corporation property .	821,959	8	0

The Bill so promoted passed its first reading
on 2nd May, the second reading on 3rd May by
a majority of 19,[1] and passed into Committee,
finally passing 10th May, and is known as 33
George III. cap. 31. This Act enabled the
Corporation of Liverpool to issue for two
years, against the deposit of approved securities, promissory notes for £5 and £10, not
bearing interest, and of £50 and £100, bearing interest, the total amount not to exceed
£300,000.

---

[1] In the minority voted John Tarleton of Liverpool, then member
for Seaford, in Sussex. In 1796 he contested Liverpool, and this vote
was then brought up against him.

The Corporation then issued the following :—

"CORPORATION LOAN OFFICE.

" To the Merchants and Inhabitants of Liverpool.

" GENTLEMEN,—The Committee for carrying into
effect the Act lately passed for issuing negotiable notes
by the Corporation, on laying before you the rules
and regulations by which the plan will be conducted
and the terms on which loans will be granted by the
Common Council, beg leave to observe that they have
framed both with a view to give every accommodation
to the public, consistent with due safety to the Corporation Estate.   This was indispensably their duty, and
they flatter themselves their endeavours to unite those
objects will be found effectual, and be viewed and
received with candour.

" The business of a Loan Office on the principles
intended by the Act is without a parallel; and there
being no institution from which the Committee could
derive information to aid their deliberations, they do
not suppose that the rules and regulations now laid
before you are the best possible ; a little experience
may point out their defects, and those defects will be
remedied and removed as they are discovered.   The
mode of obtaining a loan will be found unembarrassed,
easy, and expeditious ; the terms are as moderate as the
expenses which will unavoidably attend the institution
would permit, and fixed on that sure basis which will
protect the Corporation Estate from injury.

" It now rests with you to second the endeavours ot
the Corporation.   The inconveniences resulting from a
convulsion before unknown in the Commercial history of

this country, all have been exposed to, all have in a greater or less degree experienced : the remedy in a considerable degree is now within your power, and that is by receiving the notes to be issued in discharge of all your simple contract debts.

"That you may inspire each other with confidence in this respect, it is recommended that you signify your assent to do so publicly and without reserve. It has been suggested that this intention will be most easily collected by signing your acquiescence at Mr. Gore's shop near the Exchange.

"The notes will be ready to be issued in a few days, and notice will be given of the day on which the Public Office will be opened in the Exchange.

"The Committee, and all persons employed under them, will be bound to observe an unviolable secrecy on all applications to the Office for Loans or in any other respect.

"By order of the Committee,

"JOHN COLQUITT, *Secretary.*

"CORPORATION LOAN OFFICE,
     "LIVERPOOL, 28*th May* 1793."

The public notice of the appointment of Commissioners was as follows :—

"*Liverpool.*—At a Common Council, held in the Council Chamber, within the Exchange there, this 5th day of June 1793, being the first Wednesday in the month, pursuant to ancient custom.

"In pursuance of an Act of Parliament, made and passed in the thirty-third year of the reign of his present

Majesty, King George the III., entitled 'An Act to
enable the Common Council of the town of Liverpool,
in the County of Lancaster, on behalf and on account of
the Corporation of the said town, to issue negotiable
notes for a limited time and for a limited amount,' the
said Council do now authorise George Case, Thomas
Earle, Henry Blundell, Joseph Brooks, Thomas Naylor,
and Henry Clay, all of Liverpool aforesaid, merchants,
and Richard Statham of the same place, gentleman,
and each of them severally and respectively, to sign and
subscribe for and on behalf of the said Corporation of
Liverpool, the notes to be issued and paid by the said
Common Council, by virtue and under the powers of
the said Act of Parliament.

"COLQUITT, *Town Clerk.*

"*N.B.*—The Corporation Loan Office, in the Exchange, is open for the despatch of business, the rules
and regulations of which may be had at the said
office."

Judicious use was made of the powers thus
acquired, and the result was a great success. So
much so was it that the Loan Committee found
themselves in March of the next year in the
happy position of being able to take up notes in
their priority of date before they were due, and
public notice was given to the effect that notes
payable in June would be taken up in April,
and later a second notice stated that the notes

payable in June and July would be paid on 21st April.

On 12th March 1793 the Annual Report of the Negotiable Note Office was presented, by which it appeared that the notes issued to 25th February amounted to £140,390, and the value of the securities deposited to £155,907, 16s. 6d., and that the amount of notes then in circulation was £35,315. The Committee stated that much good had been done by the issue, and were of opinion that the Act should be extended for another three years. The extension was allowed for another year only. On 7th September 1796 the Committee presented a report preparatory to the final winding up of the operations under the Act. The loans were stated to have all been paid off, and the notes withdrawn.

The engraved forms of the promissory notes were as follows :—

No.   LIVERPOOL,   179 .

Twelve months after date I promise to pay to
          or bearer One Hundred pounds, with interest
for the same after the rate of   per cent. by the year.

                    For the Corporation of Liverpool.
£ One hundred.
Entd.

No.   LIVERPOOL,   179 .

On demand I promise to pay to   or
bearer Five Pounds, according to an Act of Parliament
passed in the thirty-third year of the reign of H*is*
Majesty King George the Third.

> For the Corporation of Liverpool.

£ Five.
Entd.

The notes for £50 and £10 were respectively
in accordance with the two forms as given above.

No 1230 Liverpool 3 March 1795

P.4225 On demand... Promise to pay to

Five Pounds

George Sterling... in Bank...

according to an... Act of Parliament passed in the thirty third

Year of the Reign of his Majesty King George the Third

I.126 for the CORPORATION of LIVERPOOL.

Tho. Taylor

Five

Ent. Redmond

John Wilson

P.143

1342

CHAPTER XII

SIR MICHAEL CROMIE, BART., POWNOLL, AND HARTMAN.

Sir Michael Cromie, Bart., Pownoll, & Hartman—Note-issuing bank — Partners — Bank dissolved — Bankruptcies of Pownoll and Hartman.

THIS bank is not mentioned in any history or directory of Liverpool that the author is acquainted with, yet its existence is abundantly attested by the survival of many of the notes issued by it, and by various legal notices relative to its bankruptcy. It is especially interesting, since it is the only genuine banking house in Liverpool that ever issued notes. When it was founded is quite unknown, but reference seems to be made to it in the postscript to the second edition of Jasper Wilson's (*i.e.* Dr. James Currie) letter to William Pitt : " A bank is proposed at Glasgow, and one has been established at Liverpool, for this express purpose," *i.e.* the issue of paper currency. But this is dated 1793, and all the notes of this firm yet seen are dated 1801. If the reference is not to this house, then, accepting Dr. Currie's

statement as fact, we have another paper-issuing
house of which no record is obtainable.   In the
directory for 1796, neither the banking house
nor any of the partners individually are in any
way referred to.   As is most probable, the
partners were non - resident.   It is suggested
also that only the later issued notes of the bank
would survive, viz. those in circulation, as the
earlier ones would on suspension of the firm be
carried away or destroyed.   But this, of course,
is mere surmise.   The banking office was at the
then 25 Lord Street, on the northern side, some-
where about where the present Lord Street
Arcade is.   The same premises were occupied in
June 1801 by Felix Yaniewicz,[1] showing that by
that date the bank had ceased to be.

[1] Felix Yaniewicz, solo violinist, impresario, music and musical
instrument dealer, was a great factor in local musical life. He conducted at the local musical festivals, and there is ample testimony that
he was an excellent violinist.   He occupied the premises of the
defunct banking company for some years.   By 1811 the firm had
become Yaniewicz & Green.   By 1818 he had taken premises on the
south side of Lord Street, then numbered 60, and had as a partner
Willoughy D. Gaspard Weiss.   The latter was a flute player.   His
son, born 2nd April 1820, was Willoughby Hunter Weiss, who was
celebrated as a bass singer in oratorio, and who composed about 1854
the extraordinarily popular setting of "The Village Blacksmith."
He died 24th October 1867.   A recent memory of his voice appears in
H. Klein's "Thirty Years of Musical Life in London" (London,
Heinemann, 1903), when he pictures the Principal of Opie House
School, Norwich, describing to his boys (1863-4 ?) "the remarkable
voice he had heard in the bass solos of the 'Messiah,'" the famous
Weiss.   The firm continued at 60 Lord Street till 1827, when, on
31st August, they gave notice that they removed from that address to

SIR MICHAEL CROMIE & CO.'S TEN-GUINEA PROMISSORY NOTE

The partners were Sir Michael Cromie, Bart., Philemon Pownoll, and Isaac Hartman.

Sir Michael Cromie was son of William Cromie, a merchant in Dublin, and second son of William Cromie of Cromore, co. Meath. William Cromie of Dublin married a Miss Fish, and had two daughters and two sons, Michael, the heir, and John, in Holy Orders. Michael was for some time M.P. for Ballyshannon, and was created a baronet of Ireland on 25th July 1776, being then described as of Stacumine, Kildare. He married Gertrude, only surviving daughter and heiress of Ford Lambert, fifth Earl of Cavan. She died 3rd May 1796, in her thirtieth year, leaving one son, William Lambert Cromie, and a daughter, who married Witney Melbourne West, Esq.

Philemon Pownoll is described in his bankruptcy notice as of Piccadilly, London, banker,

2 Church Street (late Mr. Hadwen's Bank). This was the second time in the history of the firm that they occupied the premises of bankrupt bankers. Picton ("Memorials of Liverpool," vol. ii. p. 158) says the concern was discontinued about 1828. This was not so. Felix Yaniewicz was called to Edinburgh to conduct the Gentlemen's Concerts, but his partner, Weiss, continued for many years as sole proprietor of the firm at 2 Church Street. He appears at the same place in the directory for 1845. His will was proved at Chester 1st July 1853. But an offshoot of the business arose before 1832. This was their principal assistant, James Smith, who acquired part of the business, and opened premises at 67 Lord Street, and in this year of grace 1905 the premises and business of James Smith & Son are known to every musical Liverpudlian. Felix Yaniewicz had a son of the same name, who was a dentist in Bold Street, and who in 1849 was President of the Liverpool Library.

but he is not to be found in any London directory between 1790 and 1800.[1]

He had interests in several Liverpool firms. A meeting was called for 9th April 1802 at the offices of Messrs. Lace & Hassall, Liverpool, of the "Creditors of the several firms wherein Mr. Pownoll was lately a partner."

Of Isaac Hartman all that is known is that he was a merchant, having estates in the West Indies.

On the affairs of the bank becoming involved Sir Michael Cromie escaped to France, where he lived many years. As his son, William Lambert, succeeded to the baronetcy in 1824, it is reasonable to suppose that Sir Michael died in that year.

Sir William had married in 1816 Anne Rachel, only child of Sir William Hicks, Bart., but died *s.p.* in 1841, when the title became extinct. The entailed estates went to Rev. William Cromie of Ardmorance, co. Mayo, son of Sir Michael's brother John, who had married Emily Juliana Browne, daughter of Lord Kilmaine.

The other partners were not so fortunate. A

---

[1] It is a very uncommon name, and in the endeavours to trace him correspondence was entered into with A. S. Dyer, Esq., of 98 Constantine Road, Hampstead, N.W., who kindly sent a pedigree of the Pownoll family, showing Philemon Pownolls from 1608 to 1780, the last named being Captain Philemon Pownoll, who was slain 15th June 1780 aboard the *Apollo*, which was in pursuit of a French frigate. But no further progress has been made.

SIR MICHAEL CROMIE & CO.'S ONE-GUINEA PROMISSORY NOTE

Liverpool Bank

No 122

Promise to pay the Bearer on Demand
ONE GUINEA Value received LIVERPOOL 23d day of Feby 1801

For Sir Michael Crame Bart.
Pownall & Hartman WC

One Guinea.
Entd ThRobinson

commission of bankruptcy was issued, 9th March 1802, against Philemon Pownoll, but it was not until 12th April 1808 that bankruptcy was effected in the case of Isaac Hartman, "late of Liverpool, banker, but now a prisoner in the King's Bench (late partner with Sir Michael Cromie, Bart., and Philemon Pownoll)." Affairs dragged on with the usual slowness. No mention is anywhere made as to the amount of the liabilities, but sundry dividends were paid on Philemon Pownoll's estate, the final one being 15th January 1813. Hartman, on his bankruptcy, made an offer of 8s. in the £, which does not appear to have been accepted, as in the following year his creditors again met to consider "the nature of the proposition made by Isaac Hartman to settle with them." [1]

The notes issued by this ephemeral bank are very well executed. On the left, at the top, is a vignette of the Liverpool Town Hall, on the right boldly ornate lettering, "Liverpool Bank." So far as the writer knows they are of two denominations only, one guinea and ten guineas, and for each the letterpress is different. In case of the one guinea it reads, "I promise to pay

---

[1] Living, as he did, under the privileges of the rules of the King's Bench, the creditors had no power to compel him to give up his property. It rested entirely with the debtor whether he chose to compromise with his creditors, or to live in security on what property was left to him.

the Bearer on demand "; in that of the ten guinea, " I promise to pay Mr.   or Bearer on Demand."   The author has two specimens of the guinea note, each dated 23rd February 1801, and the signatories to the notes must have been kept well employed on that day, for one is numbered 122, and the other 4226.

Beneath the vignette on the ten-guinea note it is stated that it was engraved by Yates, Liverpool. This is Samuel Yates, whose shop in Lord Street was next door to this bank.   The firm later became the well-known one of Yates & Hess, stone, seal, and copperplate engravers.   Many of the notes are signed, on behalf of the partners, by George Browne, who has been surmised to be identical with the father of Mrs. Hemans. This appears to be without sufficient foundation. Rather more probable it is that he was one of the scions of the house of Kilmaine, into which Sir Michael Cromie's brother John had married.   On the other hand, we are well assured that the J. King who signed some of the notes is Joseph King, bookkeeper and accountant, whose " Interest Tables " are largely used in the mercantile world of to-day.

CHAPTER XIII

RICHARD HANLY.

Richard Hanly—"Mock Corporation of Sephton "—" Records of a Liverpool Fireside "—Merchant and then banker—Deed of assignment to creditors.

THE bank which Richard Hanly opened was situate in Renshaw Street. He himself had been brought up as a banker's clerk. The first public appearance he made is recorded in the Minutes of the " Mock Corporation of Sephton" ("Sefton," by Caröe and Gordon, Longmans, 1893), where under date 3rd July 1791 the entry appears, p. 337—"Visitor: Mr. Richard Hanly of Liverpool, Banker's Clerk. After dinner Mr. Alderman Newsham proposed Mr. Richard Hanly to become a Member of this ancient Corporation, which, being seconded by Alderman Banner, he was admitted accordingly, and drank his ale at one gallant tip." He was son of Captain Richard and Jane Hanly. The latter was daughter of Mr. and Mrs. Thomas Askew of Cartmel. Mrs. Askew died 6th April 1789. The name of Captain Richard Hanly's father is unknown:

his mother died 17th December 1794, in her
eighty-first year, her husband having predeceased
her.   She had also a daughter, who was married,
6th June 1775, to Captain Parry, in the West
Indian trade.   In this trade also, a euphemism
for the slave trade, was Captain Richard Hanly.
As early as 1770 we find him recorded as captain
of the *Liberty* at Barbados, with 447 slaves from
Bonny.   He was a very prominent member of
that "Liverpool Fireside" whose records have
been preserved from 1776 to 1781.   They fanci-
fully described themselves in their proclamation
as "The President and Members of the Society,
deputed by Æolus to sell winds at the Port of
Liverpool, at their office, Sign of 'The Three
Tuns,' in Strand Street."[1]

   On 25th March 1776 an entry runs, "Captain

[1] The author has been enabled by the kindness of Cyril Lockett,
Esq., to inspect this volume. The Society was almost entirely composed of captains of vessels, slavers, and privateers, with a minute lay
element of superior tradesmen in the neighbourhood. Definite sums,
which duly went for refreshment of the members, were fixed for fair
winds.   Another source of income was the subscription of each
member of 2s. 6d. to celebrate his birthday. A list of the birthdays
(the year, however, being omitted) is given of ninety-two members.
Likewise each new suit of clothes, or single garment, had tribute laid
on it.

   The hostess of the "Three Tuns," at 31 Strand Street, was Mary
Catherwood.   In that very rare volume, "Williamson's Liverpool
Memorandum Book for 1753," occurs, among the list of captains
in the West India trade, the name of Alexander Caterwood as master
of a vessel. It is suggested that the widow of a former skipper would
be likely to obtain the support of his former associates and their
friends.

Richard Hanly has paid for a fair wind 3s. May he prosper. Sailed this day." It must have been an amazing sight to see these rough priva-teersmen, decked out in all their finery, meeting at their "Club" at the close of each voyage. Captain Hanly's taste was mild compared with that of many members. His suits were simple in colour, "green suit of cloaths," "chocolate coloured clothes," "blue clothes," "sage green clothes with white silk." Other gentlemen pre-sent sported garments of all the colours of the rainbow, "crimson clothes," sky-blue, maroon, &c. One gentleman had "blue coat, with hell-fire waistcoat, and thunder and lightning breeches," another, "brown coat, with black collar and yellow buttons, velvet breeches and waistcoat."

Captain Hanly's birthday was celebrated each 7th September, but an entry runs under date 14th September 1779: "The gentlemen present have this day drank Captain Richard Hanly's health for his birthday 7th inst., and a speedy release to him from his present confinement in France."

He was not kept long, however, for we find his reappearance at the club duly noted on 1st June 1780. When on shore he lived at 9 Williamson Square, showing him to be possessed of some of this world's goods.

When he died has not been traced, but by

1790 Mrs. Hanly appears as a widow. She died 26th May 1809. He had three sons: (1) Richard, the subject of this notice; (2) Thomas Askew Hanly, who became an attorney, with his office in 1796 at 9 Elbow Lane, and in 1800 at 3 Marshall Street, Lord Street, and living with his mother in Houghton Street: he disappears from mention by 1807; (3) Francis, the youngest, who died 10th February 1800 at his brother's house in Renshaw Street, aged 23.

He had also a daughter, Jane, who married, 7th April 1807, Thomas Payne of Orrell.

Richard Hanly, after the death of his father, commenced business as a merchant at 28 Renshaw Street.

He married, 3rd November 1794, a Miss Stuart. By 1803 he is described as a banker. But on 8th October 1807 he executed a deed of assignment in favour of his creditors, and two years later a first dividend was declared on his estate. Other dividends were paid, the last noted being in 1818. He retired to Orrell, where, on 14th June 1810, his wife died, aged 40, and here he himself died, 3rd February 1820.

THOMAS LEYLAND

CHAPTER XIV

LEYLAND AND BULLINS.

THE creator of this noted bank was Thomas
Leyland, born in 1752. His father was Richard
Leyland of Knowsley, of whom nothing is known.
As early as 1774 Thomas Leyland was in busi-
ness with Gerald Dillon as a partner, under the
style of Dillon & Leyland, at the lower end of
Water Street. They were in the Irish trade,
dealing in oats, peas, wheat, oatmeal, bacon, hogs'
lard, &c. They had a moderate but progressive
business, but in 1776 they had a stroke of luck.
They drew a prize of £20,000 in the lottery.
Under date 27th December 1776, Williamson's
Advertiser gives it thus: "No. 52,717 drawn on
Saturday last a prize of £20,000 is the property
of Messrs. Dillon & Leyland, merchants in this

town." [1]   Profiting by his good fortune, Leyland, on 14th May of the following year, married at St. Thomas's Church, Ellen, daughter of the late Edward Bridge.   He appears to have taken a house in Houghton Street, then a residential street.

The following year, 1778, Christopher Bullin, a Staffordshire ware merchant, at that time resident in Mathew Street, with his warehouse in York Street, became bankrupt.   He formerly resided in Duke Street, and afterwards at the centre of the pottery business, Shaw's Brow (now William Brown Street).   He had married Margaret, Thomas Leyland's sister, and Leyland appears to have had a great regard for the members of this family.   Bullin appears to have owned the house in Duke Street, with the warehouses extending along York Street to Henry Street.   Whether Leyland, at the enforced sale in 1778, bought these premises is not known, but certainly a little later they were in his hands, and here he resided for many years.

In 1779 we find Dillon & Leyland taking a two-sixteenth share in the privateer *Enterprise* of F. Ingram & Co. (see Staniforth, Ingram, & Co.),

---

[1] In the MS. "Records of a Liverpool Fireside," 1775-81, this news was given at the meeting held 23rd December 1776, but the number of the ticket there given is 44,696. Under the date 21st December the same number is given in Gore's "Annals of Liverpool," but the names of the fortunate recipients are not specified.

and they supplied the beef, pork, &c., for the
cruises.

In 1780 Thomas Leyland was elected to the
Chamber of Commerce, and on 30th September
of that year he dissolved partnership with Gerald
Dillon.

The scope of his business, now in Nova Scotia,
Liverpool, increased after this, and by 1788 we
find him a large trader in olive oil from Spain,
Peruvian bark, sherry, Tent & Carlow wines in
butt and hogshead, Ross ox mess beef in tierces,
mess pork in barrels, butter, hides, oats, and
white herrings in barrels. Later on he embarked
largely in the African slave trade, and amassed
huge sums as his profits on this cruel traffic.
When in the midst of his largest enterprises
in this direction, and consequent gains, he, in
1802, entered into partnership with the existing
bank of Clarkes & Roscoe. It was a strange
coalition: the successful slaver and the consistent opponent of slavery! Be that as it
may, it nevertheless was a powerful help to
Clarkes & Roscoe, help both material and in-
tellectual, for no keener business brain than
Thomas Leyland's was then in Liverpool, and
his wealth was patent.

It has been mentioned before that Leyland
had acquired the property at the corner of Duke
Street and York Street. His counting-house

was behind this in Henry Street, and from here
he conducted his large concerns. On 6th September 1802 appeared an advertisement that
Walton Hall, formerly the home of the Ather-
tons, an old Liverpool family who had recently
migrated to Ludlow, "a Residence admirably
suited for a commercial Gentleman of the first
importance," was for sale. Leyland rightly considered that he filled the requisite condition, and
so promptly bought the estate. Previously to
this he had been co-opted, 5th October 1796,
a member of the Town Council, and the same
year was elected Bailiff. In 1798 he was chosen
as Mayor. At the period when such honours
as the town could offer were at his disposal,
Thomas Leyland was extending vastly his operation in the African slave trade, and acquired a
spendid income from this source. His partners
in this business were his nephew, Richard Bullin,
and Thomas Molyneux, but in one venture his
partner was William Brown. The well-armed
African traders in many instances carried letters
of marque, and increased their profits by capturing
the ships of national enemies.

In 1802 he entered on the profession of a
banker, becoming senior in the then existing firm
of Clarkes & Roscoe. He quitted them suddenly,
the circular announcing the dissolution being
dated 31st December 1806, and commenced

THE RESIDENCE OF THOMAS LEYLAND, AND THE BANK AND WAREHOUSE
OF LEYLAND & BULLINS, YORK STREET, 1807

business as a banker on 10th January 1807 on
his own account in York Street, in a building
separate from, but adjacent to, his office in
Henry Street. The same year he endeavoured
to sell the Duke Street and Henry Street property, from which one may hazard the speculation that henceforward Thomas Leyland might
be known as a banker rather than as a merchant.
There was then no sale of the property, nor for
many years after, for in 1815 we find it again
offered for sale. The title of the new firm was
Leyland & Bullin, the partner being his nephew,
Richard.

In 1809 an event took place which had a very
important bearing on the after proprietorship
of the bank. This was the marriage, at Walton,
on 28th September, of Dorothy, daughter of the
late Christopher Bullin and niece of Thomas
Leyland, to John Naylor of Hartford Hill,
Cheshire, whose uncle, Thomas Naylor, was
Mayor in 1796, and during whose year of office
the present supporters to the arms of the city
were granted by George III., and added to the
arms of the town.

About this time his other nephew, Christopher
Bullin, was admitted to partnership, and the title
of the firm now became LEYLAND & BULLINS,
a title borne proudly and unsmirched for ninety-
four years, until, in 1901, under the pressure

of modern tendencies, the bank amalgamated with the North and South Wales Bank Limited.

In 1814 Thomas Leyland was again elected Mayor. During the hard times of the peace which followed after the battle of Waterloo, when the industries which had been necessary in time of war failed for want of occupation, when the inflated prices and consequent high wages ceased, and the working population felt the revulsion most, there was no more strenuous supporter of the rights of the people against the oppression of the middleman than Thomas Leyland. Whether he remembered his own early struggles, or whether his sense of justice was keen, we do not know. But for the engrosser, the forestaller, the regrater[1] he had no mercy. He, during his mayoralty of the memorable year 1814–15, made his name a terror to these evil-doers. Thomas Leyland was accustomed to visit the markets personally, and brought to justice those guilty of these offences.

Christopher Bullin does not seem to have taken any part in the slave ventures or in local political life. But it was quite different with his elder brother, Richard. As mentioned above,

---

[1] An engrosser was one who bought large quantities of market supplies in order to influence the price in the open market; the forestaller, one who bought provisions before they came to market in order to raise the price; the regrater was one who bought and sold provisions in the same market, thus raising the price.

CHRISTOPHER BULLIN

he had shares with his uncle in the slavers, and
with him he had cravings for public life. Hence
we find him co-opted on 4th January 1815 to
the Common Council.

For a great number of years he and Christopher had lived together at a house, then
12 Bold Street, a little above the Lyceum. But
by 1810 Christopher Bullin had removed to
Parliament Street, occupying one of the large
houses opposite St. James' Church. By 1815
Richard had acquired a residence at Fazakerley,
and he is described as of that place in the
nomination for the Council. It is typical of
the intensely *local* nature of the directories of
the period that they do not register him as
of Fazakerley till 1825.

In 1816 Leyland & Bullins removed to their
new premises in King Street. Their circular,
dated 28th January of that year, is as follows:
" Leyland & Bullins beg leave to inform their
friends that the banking establishment at present carried on in York Street will be removed
to their new premises in King Street on
Monday, 5th February." On 18th May of the
same year a presentation of a piece of plate,
value £500, modelled and ornamented after
the celebrated Roman vase at Warwick Castle,
was made to Thomas Leyland by a number
of Liverpool merchants, William Brown (after-

wards Sir William Brown, Bart.), as representative merchant, making the presentation.

When Canning, then member for Liverpool,
returned from fulfilling the post of Ambassador
to Madrid, he was appointed President of the
Board of Control. This necessitated his re-
election for Liverpool. Mr. Leyland was approached by the Whigs, but declined to stand.
In spite of this he was nominated, and the
election dragged on for four and a half days,
with the result: Canning, 1260; Leyland, 732.
Canning characterised it as "a struggle with
an invisible phantom."

About 1817 Anfield House seems to have
been acquired by Christopher Bullin as a
country residence. This many years later was
the residence of George Arkle, a subsequent
partner in the firm.

In 1820 Thomas Leyland was elected Mayor
for the third time, and in the following year
Richard Bullin was honoured with the mayoralty,
after a four days' contest. He was appointed
J.P. for the county on 2nd February 1824.

On 29th May 1827 Thomas Leyland died,
aged seventy-five years. His will, dated 1st
April 1822, and proved at Chester, 11th
January 1828, made the following provisions :—
After specific bequests to his widow, Ellen, his
nephews Richard and Christopher Bullin, and

others, including some few charitable bequests,
he willed that his property should go to the
lawful male heirs of his nephews Richard and
Christopher, and failing issue to the male heirs
of his niece, Dorothy Naylor, Thomas, John,
and Richard Naylor. The value of the estate
was sworn under £600,000. From the will we
gather that he had bought Fazakerley Hall,
offered for sale at the bankruptcy of Joseph
Hadwen (*q.v.*). He also bequeathed £100 to
Professor Smyth of Cambridge, son of Thomas
Smyth (*q.v.*).

Thomas Leyland was both J.P. and D.L.
for the county of Lancaster. He was, to
quote "The Old Stager," "a man of amazing
shrewdness, sagacity, and prudence. . . . We
will not compare him to the animals which
are said 'to see the wind,' but, by some intui-
tion, instinct, or presentiment, call it what you
will, he seemed always to have a warning of
any coming storm in the money market, and
trimmed and steered the ship, and took in sail
accordingly. He was a fine-looking man, with
what some thought a stern and forbidding, but
what we should call a firm and decided, look."

Though possessed of great wealth, it was
currently reported that he was extremely par-
simonious, and the squibs, during the parliamentary elections for which Thomas Leyland

M

was nominated, but for which he declined to stand, unhesitatingly attribute his reluctance to sheer stinginess, which grudged the large expenses then necessary.

But he had no sympathy with hole-and-corner work with reference to the Corporation finance. To his credit be it said that during his second tenure of the office of Mayor in 1815 he published for the first time the Corporation accounts, stating that the Mayor should lay before the burgesses an account of their money transactions. He also then caused the accounts for the seventeen years preceding to be published for their perusal.

Contemporaries credit him with a saying, which the writer's memory tells him, though unable to give the reference, was used by one greater than he (? Talleyrand), but which his extensive experience as thrice Mayor of Liverpool would bring home to him : " Many of those you invite soon forget it : those you don't invite, never forget it."

The business was now conducted under the old style by Richard and Christopher Bullin. The *Gazette* of 30th June 1827 contains licence and authority to Richard Bullin, Esq., of Warbreck House, Fazakerley, to assume the name and bear the arms of Leyland in compliance with the conditions of the will of his late maternal uncle, Thomas Leyland, bearing date 1st April 1822.

Christopher Bullin still abstained from any public life, but Richard was keenly interested in local matters. At the contest in 1827 for the mayoralty between Nicholas Robinson and Thomas Colley Porter, when bribery of the most extensive kind was openly and unblushingly practised by both sides, it was stated that he subscribed £6000 to Nicholas Robinson's expenses.

In 1835 currency was given to a story in several of the Liverpool papers, which I reproduce in Sir James Picton's words : " The banking account of the Corporation up to this time had been kept with the banking house of Messrs. Leyland & Bullins. At a meeting of the Finance Committee, held on June 19th, Alderman Leyland announced that he would make no further advances to the Corporation, the account then standing to their debit in the sum of £12,800. Some rather high words ensued. Alderman Sandbach, Conservative though he might be, was jealous for the honour of the Corporation, and immediately signed a cheque on his bankers, Messrs. Heywood & Co., for the amount. The day following the account of the Corporation was transferred from Leylands & Co. to Messrs. Heywood, where it has ever since remained." [1]

It is a very pretty story, and gives doubtless the reason why the Corporation account was

[1] " Memorials of Liverpool," vol. i. 462, ed. 1875.

closed with Leyland & Bullins, but it does not quite fit with facts.

The Corporation account was with Gregsons and Clay till their suspension in 1807. After that no public mention is made of the account, that the author is aware of, till the Parliamentary Enquiry into the Corporation was held in 1833. From that report we find that the Corporation had accounts with both A. Heywood, Sons, & Co. and Leyland & Bullins, and that the indebtedness was fairly equally distributed. On 18th October 1832 the balance due by the Corporation to A. Heywood, Sons, & Co. was £16,573, 0s. 9d., and at the end of twelve months it had increased to £29,778, 9s. 6d. For the same dates the balances due to Leyland & Bullins were £16,639, 16s., and £29,898, 18s. 6d. Evidently, therefore, the Corporation had extensive dealings with Heywoods' prior to 1835.[1]

[1] There is a curious error in Baines' "History of Lancashire," vol. iv. p. 134, London, 1836. The amount of indebtedness to Heywoods' is given as £29,898, 19s. 6d., and to Leyland's £59,677, 8s. But if the column in which these figures appear is added up, there will be found a trifling difference of £29,898, 18s. 11d. As this is, within a few pence, the indebtedness to Leyland's, it appears probable that the account from which Baines took his figures originally stood thus:—

Due to Heywoods'	.	.	.	£29,778	9	6
,, Leyland's	.	.	.	29,898	18	6
Together	.	.	£59,677	8	0

and that Baines took the latter two amounts instead of the first two.

JOHN NAYLOR

The widow of Thomas Leyland, Ellen, died
on 18th January 1839, and Richard Leyland
then took up his residence at Walton Hall,
where he died unmarried on the 1st December
1844.   Christopher Bullin retired from the
firm in 1847, and died, also unmarried, at his
residence, Upper Parliament Street, 4th September 1849.   He had assumed by Royal
Licence, on 8th May 1845, the name and arms
of Leyland.

The business of the bank was then continued
by the surviving partners, Thomas Leyland's
grand-nephews, John Naylor and Richard Christopher Naylor.   Their mother, Dorothy, died
8th December 1856, aged seventy-five years.

Richard Christopher Naylor retired in 1852,
and John Naylor then took into partnership
George Arkle (who, born 28th October 1814,
had entered the bank as an apprentice, became
managing partner, retired in 1879, and died
13th December 1885), and in 1867 Benjamin
Arkle, who died 22nd September 1891.

In 1879 John Naylor admitted his three sons,
Christopher John Naylor (who in 1891 succeeded
to the Leyland entailed estates, and took the
name of Leyland in substitution for that of
Naylor), Rowland Edward Leyland Naylor, and
John Naylor, now a director of the North and
South Wales Bank, and also John Willan

Heblethwaite (whose ancestor, Captain Heblethwaite, finds mention in the " Records of a
Liverpool Fireside "), who like the Arkles had
entered the bank as an apprentice, and who
died in 1900.   John Naylor died on the 13th
July 1889, and in 1895 the head office of the
bank was removed to new premises at 36 Castle
Street, and in May 1901, as before stated, the
bank was amalgamated with the North and
South Wales Bank Limited.

CHAPTER XV

John Aspinall & Son—Transition from tea-dealers to bankers—
Bankruptcy—James Aspinall, banker—James Aspinall & Son—
Central Bank of Liverpool.

THE first mention of this firm in the local
directory is in 1796, when, under the title of
John Aspinall & Sons, Grocers, they had their
shop at 5 Derby Square, with a warehouse at
40 Castle Street. The site of the Derby Square
premises was later on occupied by Thomas
Kaye for the *Liverpool Courier* printing works,
and is now covered by the head office of the
North and South Wales Bank Limited.

They had in 1793 a shop at the top of Dale
Street, but at the latter end of that year removed
to the corner of Derby Square and Castle Street.
The firm was composed of John Aspinall, the
father, and James and William, the sons. On
6th February 1797 they notified the public that
they " have also opened the Grocery and Tea
Warehouse in Castle Street lately occupied by
Mr. [James] Wright." This was numbered 16
in 1796. It is noteworthy that in several of

their public notices they describe their principal business premises as situate "corner of Market Place," although the newer name, "Derby Square," had been in use for many years. As was the custom, they lived over their premises in Castle Street. But on 2nd September 1796 James Aspinall married, at Leyland, Margaret Broxup of Euxton, near Chorley, and he took up his abode above the one of their business premises which was about where Messrs. Nixon and Thew's premises now stand. To this tea, &c., business gradually attached itself a banking business, and the two seem to have prospered, for in 1802–3 we find that they built " several spacious and elegant stone dwellings " on the west side of the north end of Everton Terrace. In one of these John Aspinall, the senior of the firm, went to reside.

By 1811 James Aspinall had bought and was residing at No. 28 Clare Street, corner of Islington, which had some land attached to it. His mother died at Everton on 27th May of this year, aged 71, and his wife did not long survive, dying 20th July 1813, in her thirty-ninth year.

On 9th August 1813 the Aspinalls circularised their friends :—

" John, James, and William Aspinall beg to inform their friends and the public that a dissolution of partnership has this day taken place in their house, and that the

Grocery business will be continued by William Aspinall
only, on his own account, at the established shop in the
Market· Place, corner of Derby Square. The banking
business will be continued by John and James Aspinall
only, under the firm of John Aspinall & Son, at their
present situation in Castle Street, corner of Harrington
Street, where all accounts of their late concern will be
received and paid."

James Aspinall did not remain long a widower,
as he on 12th August 1814 married, at Edgehill,
Miss Hardwick of Everton Terrace.

But the conclusion of the Napoleonic wars,
pricking the bubble of credit, brought woe to
many, amongst others to the Aspinalls.

A commission of bankruptcy, dated 27th June
1816, was issued against "John Aspinall and
James Aspinall of Liverpool, bankers." The
Liverpool Mercury thus announced it the following day : " Amongst the innumerable melancholy
tokens of the times, we are concerned to state
the stoppage of the bank of Messrs. James (should
be *John*) Aspinall & Son of this town." The
Receiver appointed was Harmood Banner,[1] to
whom thus fell his first appointment as liquidator of a bank.

1 He had previously been in partnership with his brother-in-law
under the firm of Banner & Billinge, porter dealers, 8 Lower Castle
Street. He married, 25th October 1808, at St. George's Church,
Anne, daughter of Thomas Billinge, printer, publisher, and proprietor of the *Liverpool Advertiser*. He commenced business as an
accountant in October 1814.

When going into their assets it was found
that their houses in Everton had been conveyed
to their London correspondents, Fry & Chapman,
doubtless as security for advances made. But
James Aspinall had a life interest in two farms
and other lands, with three cottages, at Euxton,
near Chorley, all of which probably came to him
through his first wife. He had also his house
and land in Clare Street. The firm held two
houses in Castle Street, Corporation lease, partly
in use as the bank, and sundry small properties.

The liquidation dragged on for many years,
several small dividends being paid, the first of
2s. 6d. in the £ early in 1817. John Aspinall
died 3rd February 1823, aged 75. In addition
to his two sons he had daughters. The eldest
married, 27th October 1799, Edward Evans;
another, Mary, died unmarried 28th May 1834.

James Aspinall reverted to his old business
as a tea and spice dealer, with the business place
in Castle Street, at the corner of Harrington
Street, and continued to live in Clare Street.
This lasted for some years, until in 1823 he
again blossomed out as a "banker," the banking
office being in Harrington Street. By 1827 he
had removed the bank to Temple Court, whence
in 1828 he respectfully acquainted his friends
that owing to the stoppage of his London correspondents, Messrs. Fry & Chapman, he had

arranged with Messrs. Drewett & Fowler, bankers, London, for future business. His own career, however, shortly received a check, for in the *Gazette* for 12th June 1832 he is declared a bankrupt.[1] But in June 1833 this bankruptcy was annulled. Then a circular from Temple Court, 10th July 1833, notifies us that "James and Broxup Aspinall respectfully inform their friends that they have commenced business together, under the firm of James Aspinall & Son, and that the account is with Sir James Esdaile & Co., bankers, London."

The joint-stock mania was very prevalent at this time. Banks were springing up in every direction, people were readily subscribing capital, and every one was to make his or her fortune in a few years. The Aspinalls thought that they too would invite the public to share their good fortune, so the Central Bank of Liverpool was duly floated on 1st August 1836, with a capital of £50,000 nominal in £10 shares, with its offices in Temple Court, and its manager James Aspinall. But even the credulous public of that date did not quite swallow the bait. Thus by 4th March 1837 the amount of the paid-up capital was only £5790.

---

1 On 17th July 1831 there had been a burglary committed on the Temple Court premises, whereby Aspinalls' lost £800 in cash, and bills to a large amount.

Their former London agents, Esdaile & Co., collapsed in 1837, but the Central Bank of Liverpool appears to have transferred its agency to Lubbock & Co. ere this.   By 1839 the bank has disappeared from the directory, and the writer has been unable to trace when or how it vanished.   The name of James Aspinall is also absent.   The name of his son is given, but by 1841 that too has gone.

CHAPTER XVI

MOSS, DALES, AND ROGERS.

Moss, Dales, & Rogers—Thomas Moss—Thomas and John Moss—John Moss—Formation of the bank—Partners—Moss, Dale, Rogers, and Moss—Erection of bank building—Moss, Rogers, & Moss—Liverpool and Manchester Railway—Thomas Edwards-Moss and Gilbert Winter Moss—North-Western Bank—London City and Midland Bank Limited.

THE founder of this bank was John Moss, whose grandfather was John Moss of Hurst House, and his father Thomas Moss of Whiston, both of which places are situate between Liverpool and Prescot. The latter came to Liverpool and was apprenticed to Thomas Case,[1]

---

[1] Thomas Case was an eminent merchant of Liverpool. He was son of Thomas Case of Red Hazles, near Prescot, who had married Margaret, daughter of William Clayton, sometime M.P. for Liverpool. He was in partnership with his aunt, Sarah Clayton, as coal merchants under the style of Clayton, Case, & Co. He also, in 1774, was in partnership with William Gregson as insurance brokers under the style of Gregson, Case, & Co. The bankruptcy of the coal firm early in 1778 put an end to the insurance partnership. He married, 5th December 1776, Anna, the eldest daughter of the late John Ashton. His aunt, Sarah Clayton, was a very well-known Liverpool lady, who gave her name to the square she resided in. A contiguous street is Cases Street. She died May 1779. Thomas Case, whose name figures on the first African Committee of 1777, had two sons, both merchants of Liverpool, Thomas, afterwards Alderman Case, and John Ashton Case.

25th May 1762, and was enrolled as a freeman in 1770.

He commenced business as a timber merchant, his first firm being Taylor, Moss, & Co., the partnership in which was dissolved 15th April 1776, Thomas Moss continuing in the old yards at the east side of Salthouse Dock and bottom of Lord Street.

On 9th May 1777 he married at St. Peter's Church, Liverpool, Jane, only child of Thomas Arrowsmith, who was descended from the Cottingham family.[1]

In 1778 the new partnership he had formed under the title of Thomas Moss & Co. was dissolved, and he commenced a fresh partnership under the title of Moss, Sutton, & Co. But this was of brief duration, as in the following year it was dissolved, his partners, James Sutton and Edward Lowe, continuing the business. In 1780 he had acquired a new timber yard on the east side of St. George's Dock. In 1778 he had purchased land on the road from Liverpool to Low Hill, contiguous to that owned by Richard Gildart. The streets, Moss Street and Gildart Street, sufficiently mark the locality. Moss Street was cut through the land about 1809.

His name appears as the owner of a privateer

[1] Thomas Cottingham died at his mansion house at Ness, Cheshire, on 22nd May 1783.

during the war with America. He also developed
a business as general merchant, first in Paradise
Street, where he also resided, but latterly in
Manesty Lane. Owing to the erection of the
Goree Warehouses and Piazzas in 1793 his timber
yard was removed to the west side of St. George's
Dock.

On 26th April 1796 he married, as second
wife, Miss Griffies, the sister of William Roscoe's
wife.

In 1803 he took into partnership his son John,
the firm then becoming Thomas and John Moss.
After living for some time in Rainford Gardens
he had taken a house in the very fashionable
St. Anne Street, and here he died, 5th February
1805.

John Moss, who now succeeded to the various
businesses, general merchant, shipowner, &c.,
was born in Rainford Gardens, where his father
then resided, on 18th February 1782. On his
attaining his majority he was, as stated above,
taken into partnership with his father, and at the
early age of twenty-three he was principal of
extensive businesses. The timber business, however, was not included in these. This was taken
over by Thomas Moss's partner therein, Richard
Houghton, who continued the business for
many years, first at the old yard, west side of
St. George's Dock, later in Hurst Street.

In the same year, 1805, John Moss married
on 3rd September, at the Collegiate Church,
Manchester, Hannah Taylor, daughter of the
late Thomas Taylor of Moston.

In 1807 appeared an advertisement in Billinge's
Advertiser which the author has always, rightly or
wrongly, connected with the origin of Moss's
Bank :—

"A gentleman, possessing a large disposable property,
in correspondence with the very first house in London,
would treat with one person, of known property, to
establish a BANK at LIVERPOOL, upon the most solid
and permanent basis, by which the Public will be
guaranteed against any fortuitous event.   Letters for
A.B.C. at the Post Office, Liverpool (post paid), from
Principals, with real signatures, will be attended to, if
connexion is deemed desirable.   *N.B.*—An active part
is absolutely necessary, as *that* is the only motive for
this advertisement."

Whether the surmise be right or wrong, the
quotation is interesting in itself, as showing
the feeling that properly equipped banks were
essential to the needs of the vastly expanding
commerce of the town.

But we have the fact that John Moss in this
year opened a bank at 4 Exchange Buildings,
under the title of Moss, Dales, & Rogers.   It is
not mentioned in the body of the directory for
1807, but has a special entry in the appendix.

The Dales were Roger Newton Dale, who had married on 9th March 1802 Margaret, sister of John Moss, and George Edward Dale, who on 9th October 1804 had married Ellen, another sister of John Moss. They came from Heaton Norris, near Stockport.   R. N. Dale was a member of the firm of Davies, Dale, & Co.,[1] of Redcross Street, Liverpool, drysalters, who had their oil and paint warehouse in Redcross Street, and their manufactory at 44 Hunter Street. They were also, during the Napoleonic wars, privateer owners.   R. N. Dale lived at Wavertree, and died at his house there, 23rd February 1809, aged 33.[2]

His brother, G. E. Dale, did not long survive him, as he died at his house in Rodney Street, 9th January 1815.[3] He left several children.

[1] Early in 1808 Davies, Dale, & Co. dissolved partnership. Business was carried on at the old premises by James Davies and R. N. Dale under the style of James Davies & Co., while the other partner, Joseph Bancroft, entered into partnership with his brother-in-law, Joseph Dutton, under the style of Dutton & Bancroft.

[2] His widow went to reside at Cheltenham, but died at the house of her brother Henry in Wavertree, 15th May 1822.

[3] The widow went to Leamington, whence her second daughter, Ellen, was married, 22nd September 1831, to Rev. Hugh Matthie, Rector of Worthenbury, Flints, surviving only to 28th July 1836. The eldest daughter, Sarah Jane, was also married at Leamington on 22nd August 1833 to T. R. Woodward of Birkenhead. Mrs. Dale changed her residence to Farndon, Cheshire, where her youngest daughter, Hannah, died 7th February 1836. Mrs. Dale herself died on 28th September of the same year at the house of her son-in-law, T. R. Woodward.

The only son, Roger Newton Dale, died 18th
September 1828, in the twentieth year of his age.

The other partner was Edward Rogers. He
was, it is believed, the son of Edward Rogers, a
merchant of Liverpool, who also carried on an
insurance and brokerage business, under the title
of Rogers & Ripley. This latter firm was dissolved 31st December 1785, and Edward Rogers
carried on the business alone at 6 Change Alley.
He married at Whitehaven, 29th December
1778, a Miss Nicholson of that town, but she
did not long survive, dying June 1782.

To Edward Rogers belongs the distinction
of being the originator in 1757 of the proposal
for the formation of the Liverpool Library
(the first circulating library in the kingdom),
happily still flourishing. He died 1795. The
son of Edward Rogers took up his residence
in Everton, where he lived till about 1822,
when he removed to 2 South Hunter Street,
changing to St. Michael's Hill, Toxteth Park,
about 1831, where he continued to reside after
his retirement from the bank a few years
later.

On 5th September 1811 John Moss's younger
brother, Henry, was married at Oldham to
Hannah, second daughter of James Clegg of
Bent, and the same year he was admitted a
partner in the bank, which was now Moss,

MOSS'S BANK, DALE STREET, 1811–1864

Dale, Rogers, & Moss. In the same month was completed the building facing the Town Hall, at the end of Dale Street, which was the home of the bank until the private bank became a joint-stock concern in 1864, under the title of the North-Western Bank. The building was then reconstructed.

The press notice on the present occasion was as follows :—

16th September 1811.

"A small but very fine specimen of Doric architecture, remarkably well executed in choice freestone, is now exhibited in the building just erected at the top of Dale Street, which is said to be intended for the banking house of Messrs. Moss, Dale, Rogers, & Co. Such structures as these, in the middle of a great town, contribute greatly to the credit of, and of course to the benefit of, the place in which they are erected ; whilst they reflect honour on the taste and spirit of their proprietors."

John Moss had lived for some time at Mossley Hill, but he had now acquired, and was resident at, the estate of Otterspool. Here in 1812–13 he started an oil mill in partnership with George Forwood.[1] For many years there had been a

---

[1] George Forwood, son of Lieutenant Forwood, R.N., and Faith, his wife, was an exceedingly able man. He tried his hand at various businesses, was agent for naval varnish, general merchant, insurance agent, and overseer for the poor. He was father of George Peplow Forwood and Thomas Brittain Forwood, and grandfather of the late Sir Arthur B. Forwood, Bart., sometime Secretary to the Admiralty, and Sir William B. Forwood.

mill on the shore. The Otterspool stream formed an embouchure, which had been improved by embankments. Hence barges had direct access to the mill. In 1780 the firm of Tate, Alexander, & Wilson enclosed a part of the strand of the river Mersey and erected a snuff mill. This was continued for many years, and was held under Thomas Tarleton on lease. In 1816 John Moss purchased the interest of the lord of the manor (John Blackburn) in the strand in front of his property, and made further embankments. The oil mill was burnt down many years ago, but the embankments on a summer evening, "when softe is the sonne," make a delightful spot for rest and contemplation. Here Mersey is nearly at her widest, and the effect of the broad stretch of water, with the green and gentle slopes of Cheshire leading up to the background of the everlasting hills of Wales, the whole lighted up by a glorious sunset, is at once charming and restful.

By the death of George Edward Dale in 1815 the Dales dropped out of the title of the firm, which now became Moss, ROGERS, and Moss, and so continued till the thirties.

On 20th January 1816 John Moss was created J.P. for the county of Lancaster. In 1822 he commenced, in conjunction with some of

the best known Liverpool men, the great task
of endeavouring to obtain powers for the projected undertaking, the Liverpool and Manchester Railway. Co-operation with Manchester
was sought and obtained, and at the first meeting
of the Joint-Committee, held at George Ashby
Pritt's office, John Moss was elected Chairman.
This office he retained during the following
three years, till, on his own recommendation
in 1824, Mr. Charles Lawrence, then Mayor of
Liverpool, was solicited to join the Committee
and become its Chairman. The history of the
conflict that took place, of the unworthy
opposition of those who should have known
better, and of the interests that had to be
placated (the Bridgwater Trust took as its
bribe shares to the extent of one-fifth of the
undertaking), is out of place here. Suffice it
to say that on the first attempt to obtain
parliamentary sanction the Corporation of
Liverpool, by objecting to the proposed company taking land for its purposes, effectually
stayed for a while the progress of the undertaking.[1] But in 1825 the Bill was passed
through both Houses, and received the Royal
assent. The first meeting of the proprietors
was held in Liverpool on 29th May 1826,

---

[1] Thomas Creevey in the "Creevey Papers" plumes himself on the
fact that by his tactics he obtained this result. He was acting on
behalf of his friend, Lord Sefton.

when fifteen directors were elected, three of
whom were nominees of the Bridgwater Trust.
At the first meeting of the directors on the
following day, Charles Lawrence was elected
Chairman, and John Moss Deputy-Chairman of
the Company.

Later on John Moss identified himself with
other railway undertakings, and in 1831 was
Chairman of the Liverpool and Birmingham
Railway.

His brother Henry contented himself with
municipal matters, and was chosen a member
of the Common Council 6th October 1824.

Mercantile matters were not entirely forgotten.
John Moss had some very large sugar plantations
in the neighbourhood of Demerara.

The bank continued to prosper, and obtained
a fair share of public support.

John Moss died 3rd October 1858, and was
buried at St. Anne's, Aigburth. The land on
which the church was built had been given by
him. It was opened in 1837, and was embel-
lished by his further gift of a painted glass
window.

His two sons, Thomas and Gilbert Winter
Moss, who had been for some time associated
with their father, now continued the bank.

Two other sons of John Moss were Rev. John
James Moss, sometime Vicar of Upton, Cheshire,

SIR THOMAS EDWARDS MOSS, BART.

who died in 1865, holding a living in Somerset-
shire, and James Moss, who founded the extensive
line of steamers known as the Moss Line. The
former was the eldest son of the family.

Thomas Edwards-Moss was the second son.
He was born at Otterspool 17th July 1811.
He was educated at Eton and Oxford. The
first name in the roll of Captains of the Boats
at Eton is that of Thomas Moss, as he then
was.   He married in 1847 Amy Charlotte,
daughter and heiress of Richard Edwards of
Roby, whose name, in addition to his own,
he assumed by Royal Licence four years later.
He took a great part in Liverpool parliamentary
elections, being Chairman of the Constitutional
Association. He became J.P. and D.L. for the
county, and in 1868 was created a baronet by
Lord Beaconsfield. He died 26th April 1890.
He left two sons, John Edwards - Moss and
Tom Cottingham Edwards-Moss.[1] The former
succeeded to the baronetcy. He was born

---

[1] The school and college careers of these men exhibit a striking
example of hereditary rowing ability. Sir Thomas Edwards-Moss
was Captain of the Boats in 1828. His son John was captain in
1869, and Tom in 1873-74. In the University races John rowed for
Oxford in 1870 and 1871, but, as those were Goldie's years, his side
was not successful. Tom rowed for Oxford in 1875-6-7-8, Oxford
winning in 1875 and 1878, losing in 1876, whilst in 1877 occurred
the only dead heat on record. Only a year or two ago Sir John had
the pleasure of seeing his son John elected Captain of the Boats. In
the chapel of Brasenose College there is a window to the memory of
T. C. Edwards-Moss.

25th October 1850, and married in 1873 Margaret Everilda, daughter of Colonel John Ireland Blackburn of Hale Hall.

The other son of John Moss interested in the bank was Gilbert Winter Moss. He was not much in evidence as a public character, but was greatly esteemed for his artistic tastes and charitable bent. Born 31st March 1828, he was created a J.P. for Lancashire in 1850, and died 6th July 1899.

In April 1864 the private bank was transformed into a joint-stock concern, under the title of the North-Western Bank, Thomas Edwards-Moss and Gilbert Winter Moss becoming directors. The latter remained a director until the octopus-like tentacles of the London and Midland Bank clutched it in October 1897. Later on the latter bank became the London City and Midland Bank Limited.

GILBERT WINTER MOSS

CHAPTER XVII

JOSEPH HADWEN.

Joseph Hadwen—Tea-dealer to banker—Transmission of bank-notes
to London—Bankruptcy—Claims paid in full.

THE bank in Church Street, which was originated by Joseph Hadwen, had its origin in
the grocery and tea business. It was situate a
little beyond the present premises of Bunney's
Limited. At the time when our earliest directory was published, 1766, Joseph Hadwen, senior,
had his place of business in Church Street, then,
with this exception, a residential street. He is
then described as clockmaker, grocer, and linen
draper. Before 1796 he had retired to St.
Anne Street, leaving the conduct of the business in the hands of his son, also Joseph Hadwen. They were members of the Society of
Friends, who quite generally at this time were
referred to as "the people called Quakers."
Joseph Hadwen, senior, died 31st July 1807,
aged nearly 82. His son in the same year
appeared publicly as a banker, the bank being

conducted on the first floor, whilst the tea,
&c., business was carried on on the ground floor.
He also ceased to reside over the bank in
Church Street, going to his father's former
house in St. Anne Street. The bank progressed
quietly for many years. In 1810 Joseph Hadwen took down a windmill which he owned in
Hotham Street, and erected a charity school on
the site.

In 1823 Hadwen had a stroke of ill-luck.
He had on hand £2095 in old £1 Bank of
England notes, and forwarded them by the mail
to be collected. An insight into the times is
given us by the account of the incident. To
avert suspicion as to the nature of the contents
of the parcel the notes were not addressed to
his London agents, Barclay, Bevan, & Co., Lom-
bard Street, but to a druggist in the same
street, to be by him handed to Barclay & Co.
But on its arrival in London the contents were
found to be metamorphosed into a collection
of waste paper of all descriptions.

The direful year of 1825 claimed as one
of its victims Joseph Hadwen. His circular
announcing the fact is noteworthy:—

"It is with much regret that I have to inform
thee, that in consequence of the general pressure of
the times, together with some recent failures, I have
thought it desirable to have the advice of some dis-

interested friends relative to the situation of my
affairs.

"In pursuance of their recommendation I have
concluded upon suspending my payments, a measure
truly distressing to my own feelings, particularly so in
looking to the various embarrassments it may occasion.

"What may remain to me after paying my creditors
in full must depend upon management and circumstances unforeseen.

"JOSEPH HADWEN.

"CHURCH STREET, 1st month, 24th, 1826."

The liabilities were estimated at £120,000,
but the assets were in such a liquid condition
that dividends amounting to 12s. 6d. in the
£ were paid to the creditors before twelve
months were over. A large number of the
members of the Society of Friends banked with
Hadwen, many of those being leather and
hide dealers. The creditors were so pleased
with the favourable aspect of affairs that they
presented the assignees of the estate with a
piece of plate in recognition of their assiduity
in winding up the estate.

Among the properties belonging to Joseph
Hadwen which were brought to the hammer
were Fazakerley Hall, with outbuildings, garden, orchards and lands, amounting to 84
acres, 3 roods, 10 poles, which was bought
by Thomas Leyland; the bank in Church

Street, and his residence in St. Anne Street. The creditors were all paid in full.

In December 1826 Joseph Hadwen announced that he had gone into partnership with Elizabeth Fielden, under the style of Hadwen and Fielden, as tea and coffee dealers at the "Three Canisters" in New Scotland Road, near Great Nelson Street, N. Since 1811 Mary Fielden had conducted the tea-dealing business in Church Street beneath the bank. Stonehouse[1] says that Hadwen's sisters, "The Misses Hadwen," conducted the tea business. Possibly an explanation may be found by assuming that Elizabeth Fielden was the married name of one of the Hadwens. The directories give no clue as to whether she was maid, wife, or widow.

However, the firm of Hadwen & Fielden was in existence as late as 1845.

1 "Streets of Liverpool," p. 165, ed. 1879.

SAMUEL HOPE

CHAPTER XVIII

SAMUEL HOPE AND CO.

Samuel Hope & Co.—George Holt—Cotton brokers and bankers—
Dissolution of partnership—Edward Burrell—Liverpool Borough
Bank—Crisis of 1847—Crisis of 1857—Suspension of Borough
Bank—Methods of management.

THE founder of this firm was Samuel Hope,
son of William Hope. The latter was a
mercer and draper, living for many years at
1 Atherton Street, with his warehouse adjoining
at 14 Pool Lane (now South Castle Street).
This block of property is, I take it, repre-
sented by Plate 20 in vol. ii. of Herdman's
" Pictorial Relics of Ancient Liverpool." Here
with him resided his son Samuel, who, after
an apprenticeship with Nicholas Waterhouse,
commenced business in 1803 as a cotton broker
at 2 Water Street, on the south side immediately below Castle Street.

By 1807 William Hope[1] had retired from
business, and had built himself a house at the
corner of Hope Street and Hardman Street.

[1] He died 20th March 1827, aged 76.

Here Samuel Hope also lived. The house is now the expensively decorated Philharmonic Hotel. In the same year, 7th October 1807, he took as apprentice George Holt, aged 17. The latter, son of Oliver Holt, was born at Town Mill, Rochdale, on 24th June 1790. At the conclusion of his apprenticeship in 1812, Samuel Hope took him into partnership. The circular, dated 28th November 1812, is as follows :—

"I have pleasure to apprise you that I have taken Mr. George Holt into partnership with myself under the title of 'Samuel Hope & Co.' Having been invited to this measure by the assistance I have derived from Mr. Holt's ability and application during the five years he has been acquiring a knowledge of the business in my office, I am encouraged to hope that these qualities will powerfully second my own exertions to merit a continuance of your patronage."

To the business of cotton brokers they added later on that of bankers.

On 17th September 1816 Samuel Hope married at St. John's, Manchester, Rebecca (or Rebekah), daughter of Thomas Bateman, Esq., then of Higher Ardwick, near Manchester, but subsequently of Middleton Hall, Youlgreen, co. Derby.

On 1st September 1820 George Holt married at Edge Hill Church, Emma, the elder daughter of William and Jane Durning.[1]

Samuel Hope had purchased a considerable amount of property in Everton, and in 1820[2] he took down two excellent houses, and built on their site a stately edifice. Here, in Everton Terrace, he took up his residence, and lived there till his death. Syers,[3] speaking of the proprietor of this "spacious and elegant mansion," says, "To the poor and uneducated he has been, and still continues to be, a fervent, active, and sincere friend."

On 30th June 1823 the partnership between Samuel Hope and George Holt was terminated, the official notice of the dissolution appearing

---

[1] William Durning had been a wine and spirit merchant, with offices at first in School Lane, later on in Church Street. He had a partner, Edmund Lewin, who, after William Durning's retirement from business about 1820, carried on the firm under the title of Lewin and Lassell. Mr. Durning had for many years resided in Edge Lane, and had acquired a considerable amount of land in the neighbourhood. Hence the ancient road called Rake Lane, on which part of this property abutted, was in later years re-named Durning Road, and when a continuation road was made through other portions of Mr. Durning's land this was named Holt Road. Mr. William Durning's property went to his two daughters, one married to George Holt as above, the other to J. B. Smith, sometime M.P. for Norwich. William Durning died 4th September 1830, in his eightieth year, his wife Jane predeceasing him on 27th February 1830, aged 70 years. The date of the marriage of George Holt is wrongly given as 1821 in Gomer Williams' "Liverpool Privateers," p. 132 n.

[2] Picton gives this date as 1818, but I take it that this is a printer's error.

[3] "History of Everton," Liverpool, 1830.

in the *Gazette* for 8th May 1824. In view of the different parts enacted by the partners in connection with their joint concern as cotton brokers and bankers, it is curious to note the allocation of the businesses which now became divided. Samuel Hope, who had originated the cotton business, became banker solely, and George Holt, to whom it is said that the initiation of the banking business was due, became cotton broker solely.

Here we part with George Holt, who was eminently successful in business, and who died, full of honours, on 16th February 1861.[1]

---

[1] His wife Emma, born 20th February 1802, died 7th July 1871. George Holt was unwearied in his exertions, with heart, brain, and purse, for the improvement, whether of mind, body, or estate, of his less fortunate fellow-citizens. At a time when public opinion was, to say the least, apathetic as to the value of "secondary" education, he devoted valuable time and energy to its support. His work in furthering the objects of the Mechanics' Institution, now the Liverpool Institute, was incessant, and his purchase of Blackburne House, for the formation, in connection with the Liverpool Institute, of a Girls' Public School, proved him to be long in advance of current ideas. The building and grounds of the latter school, the first of its kind in England, were, on his decease, presented by his family to the Directors of the Liverpool Institute as a memorial of George Holt. In him the charities of the town found an unfailing friend. He also occupied himself with public affairs, being a member of the Town Council from 1835 to 1856. As Chairman of the Water Committee he conducted the difficult task of converting unlearned opposition to the Rivington Water Scheme into appreciation of its necessity. Thus was laid the foundation of Liverpool's magnificent water supply. As a member of the Dock Board, he stoutly maintained the necessity of treating its aims and objects as a national trust, rather than as of purely local concern. He was a J.P. both for borough and county.

GEORGE HOLT

He for a while continued his cotton business
next door to his old partner, but later on
removed to 1 Chapel Street, and finally occupied
part of his property, India Buildings, Water
Street. These were built in 1833, and at the
time they were erected it was considered that
their projector was erratic. But time proved
the foresight of George Holt, and his example
of erecting large blocks of mercantile offices soon
found numerous imitators.

The bank[1] still retained the title of Samuel

His sons worthily preserve the traditions of their father, the splendid
tradition of using their wealth for public weal. The motto of the
Liverpool Institute is *Non nobis solum sed toti mundo nati*, and to that
motto the Holt family gives living force. In recent years the gift,
the magnificent gift, to the community of Wavertree Park as a play-
ground for the children for ever, sufficiently stamps the thoughtfully
generous cast of mind of the Holt family. Later the purchase and
presentation of the block of property known as Sandon Terrace, to
enable the Liverpool Institute to widen its borders, gives evidence
of their strong desire that the vast school, to which their father was
so liberal and devoted, should not lack space for adequate expansion.
Still more recently the opening of the George Holt Physics Labora-
tory in Liverpool University marked another step in the same direction. This member of the family, born 9th September 1824, died 3rd
April 1896, had previously founded and endowed chairs of physiology
(1891) and pathology (1894), and was in other respects generous to
the University. It was in the fitness of things that the first Lord
Mayor of Liverpool should be Robert Durning Holt, whose name
also is the latest distinguished addition to the distinguished roll of
Liverpool's honorary freemen.

[1] Picton ("Memorials of Liverpool," vol. ii. p. 56, ed. 1875) has
stated that the house of John Tarleton, Mayor of Liverpool 1764,
was on the site of the present Manchester and Liverpool District
Bank. This the author believes to be an error.
The site of the District Bank is that of the Borough Bank, which

Hope & Co., the "Co." being Edward Burrell, who had been with Samuel Hope for some time. They prospered, and were wealthy men when, under the influence of the current mania, they converted the private bank into a joint-stock company under the title of the Liverpool Borough Bank, with a capital of £500,000 in £10 shares. They found excellent support, 32,000 out of the 50,000 shares being appropriated before the public issue. The main points of their circular to their clients are :—

"WATER STREET, LIVERPOOL,
16th June 1836.

"We have given notice by advertisement, and now particularly apprise you, of our intention to decline the

---

succeeded Samuel Hope & Co. in business and building. Now John Tarleton died in 1773, and was succeeded by his son Thomas. The position of his house can be shown by comparing the early directories :—

1774—Talbot, 7 Water Street. Thomas Tarleton, 10 Water Street.
1781— Do. 6 do. Do. 9 do.

Thus Tarleton lived below the Talbot Hotel, on the site of which the Bank of Liverpool now stands.

In 1786, when the west side of Castle Street was thrown back, the houses at the upper end of Water Street were cut off. Hence in 1790 we find the house of Daniel Dale, The King's Arms, is 5 Water Street. Now Daniel Dale, when in 1786 opening the King's Arms Hotel, advertised it as "Late the house of Thomas Tarleton." In 1829 James Brierley ("Binns Collection," vol. xiii.) sketched the "Parish Offices, late King's Arms Inn," showing it to be on the east corner of Fenwick Street. The Talbot is shown next door, higher up Water Street.

The same error is found in the note to page 280, vol. i. ed. 1875, itself a correction of a greater error in the first edition.

banking business from and after 1st July next in favour
of the Liverpool Borough Bank, of which our Mr.
Edward Burrell is appointed Manager, and Mr. Hope
the Chairman of the Board of Directors. The business
will be conducted as heretofore, and on the same
premises. . . . Grateful acknowledgments of confidence . . . during the last thirteen years.

" Samuel Hope & Co."

But the connection of the original partners
of Samuel Hope & Co. with the newly-formed
joint-stock bank did not last long. On 23rd
September 1837 Edward Burrell died in London,
aged 44. He had resided in Stafford Street from
about 1820 to 1828, removing thence to Litherland, and later, before 1832, to Orrell (if
indeed these two latter abodes be not the same
house), where his home was at the time of his
death.

He was of humble parentage, early lost his
father, and was brought up at the Kendal Blue
Coat School. He had married—when and to
whom the author has failed to find. She was
named Margaret, but they do not appear to have
had any children. His will, proved at Chester
4th November 1837, left an annuity to his mother,
Susan Troughton, wife of Richard Troughton,
Kendal, weaver, and various benefactions to
public charities, amongst them being a bequest
of 500 guineas to the Kendal Blue Coat School,

"of which institution he frequently expressed the most grateful recollection." The value of the estate was sworn under £40,000.

On 15th October of the same year Samuel Hope died at the house of his father-in-law, Thomas Bateman, Middleton Hall, near Bakewell, in his fifty-seventh year.[1] He was a man of considerable strength of character, and had pronounced Liberal views. In philanthropic endeavours he was ever to the fore, and he was earnest in his promotion of educational improvement.

When a meeting was called on 8th June 1825 to support the project of Mechanics' Institution (now the Liverpool Institute) he was one of the principal speakers. He identified himself strongly with the anti-slavery movement, and was an influential speaker at public meetings in 1829 and 1831 in connection with the agitation for the removal of restrictions on commerce caused by the exclusive charter of the East India Company. A sturdy Nonconformist, Mr. Hope took the chair on two occasions in 1837 when the question of the abolition of church rates occupied public attention.

It is to be feared that the untimely removal of the original proprietors of the bank from the

[1] His wife, Rebekah, born 12th April 1794, died on 8th October 1838. They had ten children.

supervision and management was not in favour
of the success of the joint-stock concern. As
was the case with so many others of the banks
started about this time, much imprudent business
was done, and funds were not kept liquid. In
1847 a crisis occurred, due largely to excessive
railway speculations. The locked-up state of
the Borough Bank's assets made it necessary
that the assistance of the Bank of England
should be obtained.

Ten years later came the crisis caused by the
universal distrust in America. It was there
discovered that the railway accounts had been
"cooked," and under the influence of the bad
feeling which this produced an organised "bear"
movement was made against all undertakings.
One hundred and fifty banks failed in Pennsyl-
vania, Maryland, Virginia, and Rhode Island.
The movement swelled into a panic and re-
acted on England. The nearest ports to America
first felt the shock. On 27th October 1857 the
Borough Bank closed its doors.

On examination of its affairs it was found that
its bad debts were exceedingly large. Some
£600,000 to £700,000, previously taken as good,
were now found to be almost valueless. They
had £3,500,000 bills in London with the endorsement of the bank, and of this amount some
£700,000 to £1,000,000 "had no negotiable

validity at all except that endorsement." The total loss was estimated at £940,000, the whole capital of the bank being thus swept away.

There was no question as to advances having improperly been made to favoured persons, the disasters being caused by want of discretion in the management.

Incidentally the Parliamentary Committee, appointed to inquire into the causes of the panic of 1857, revealed the former method of the management of the bank. There were twelve directors, who appointed two managing directors and a chairman. The entire conduct of the accounts was entrusted to the two managing directors and the manager, the other directors not being in touch with the customers or their accounts.

CHAPTER XIX

EVANS, CHEGWIN, AND HALL.

THE above was a firm of booksellers and stationers who had their place of business in 1816 at 14 Castle Street. Very little information is forthcoming concerning them. One of the peculiarities of the case is that only Evans and Hall are designated in the directories as "bankers and booksellers," Chegwin appearing as "bookseller and stationer" only.

The partners were Hugh Ellis Evans, Thomas Chegwin,[1] and William Eaton Hall.

Of Hugh Ellis Evans nothing is known except that he married, 13th July 1813, Miss Frances Jones, and that he for some time resided at Brownlow Hill.

William Eaton Hall was the son of Eaton and Frances Hall. Eaton Hall was an enameller in Pitt Street, where he died 21st December 1816,

---

[1] He married, 3rd August 1816, at St. George's, Everton, Mary, daughter of Sedman Parker. The last named died 14th September 1827, aged 62. He had a slight connection with the banking community, inasmuch as he took over the business of Clarke the grocer, who issued the *Liverpool Halfpenny*.

aged 67 years. His wife died 4th May 1832, aged 70 years. William Eaton Hall had been resident for some years in Russell Street. It appears that he had been a clerk with Messrs. A. Heywood, Sons, & Co.

The sole records of their banking are in the Liverpool directories, which, in successive years' describe them as " bankers and booksellers." But the dire year of 1825 came, and the names of Hugh Ellis Evans and William Eaton Hall appear no more as bankers.

They both at this time changed their residences, and both went to reside in Seymour Street.

The firm of Evans, Chegwin, & Hall as printers and stationers is given in the directories up to 1841, but in the year 1845 the title is Evans & Chegwin.

CHAPTER XX

John Threlfall—Multiplicity of businesses—Bankrupt—Stolen Bank
of England note—Threlfall's Brewery Company.

JOHN THRELFALL was originally a grocer in Kent
Square, who by 1816 had gone to reside in
Nelson Street, St. James, and by 1818 had expanded into a variety of businesses. He then
resided at 8 Nelson Street, and had a bank,
wholesale grocery warehouse, and liquor vaults
at 8 York Street. A considerable business was
done, but on 10th January 1824 a commission in
bankruptcy was issued against him. A list of his
businesses appear, and they are sufficiently varied
—brewer, liquor merchant, grocer, spirit dealer,
bill-broker, banker, &c. One wonders what was
covered by that " &c."

He held a large amount of freehold and lease-
hold property in Liverpool, and an interest in a
steam corn-mill, at that time a great novelty.
He also had a freehold estate of 60 acres,
with farmhouse, buildings, &c., at Whittingham,
between Lancaster and Preston.

His London correspondents were Williams and Co., with whom he turned over £200,000 per annum, no inconsiderable sum in those days.

Later on in the year 1824 an action was brought against him for discounting a Bank of England note for £1000 which had been stolen. Threlfall had discounted it for a Jewish slop-seller named Isaac Henry, of Pool Lane, keeper of an American tavern. Scarlett, K.C., led for the prosecution, and he gave the rough edge of his tongue to bankers such as Aspinall and Threlfall, drawing very invidious distinctions between their businesses and those of Moss, Heywood, and Leyland. It appeared that the note was first offered to Aspinalls' for discount, who said *that they had not so much money in the place*. A verdict of £1000 and 40s. costs was entered against John Threlfall.

His estate realised considerable dividends.

He continued in the liquor line of business, establishing himself in Crosbie Street, Park Lane, the site of which is now covered by the London and North-Western Wapping Goods Station. He next became a wine merchant in Cornwallis Street, afterwards at the same place a provision merchant.

A John Mayor Threlfall, ale and porter brewer, whom it is presumed was his son, resided with him here, and had a brewery at 3 and 4 Crosbie Street aforesaid.

John Threlfall's wife died 12th September 1826, aged 53. They had a daughter, Alice, who was married 17th April 1823 to Samuel Antwiss of Aston, Cheshire.

John Mayor Threlfall about 1832 commenced his brewing business in Crosbie Street, and until 1847 it continued there, in which year he had established a supplementary brewery in Trueman Street. By 1862 he had opened a brewery in Manchester. He died between then and 1864, and his executors continued the three breweries. By 1866 the address of the Manchester brewery was Cook Street, Salford. It was registered as a limited liability company on 16th March 1888, and was thus formed to amalgamate the businesses of J. M. Threlfall and W. A. Matheson. The present capital paid up is £1,825,000.

CHAPTER XXI

ROBERT FAIRWEATHER.

THE author is unable to give any account of this banker. He is in the directory of 1818 described as being a banker residing at 34 Ranelagh Street, in 1821 as of 60 Ranelagh Street, and in 1823 as of 2 Cases Street, but in 1825 he is described as a "gentleman" of 2 Cases Street.

He was the son of Patrick and Ellen Fair-weather. The former went through the usual gradations of slaver captain, privateer captain, privateer owner, finally settling down on shore as a merchant.

We find that his ship *Dalrimple*, which had sailed from Liverpool for Old Calabar on 20th October 1772, was in the following March ashore on the Isle of May.

His employers, Bolden & Co., gave him the command of the *Bellona*, 250 tons, 24 guns, and 140 men, and with her he took several prizes, one, which he took into Jamaica in 1780, being worth £4000.

In 1790 he was master of the ship *Mary Anne*.

By 1798-9 he is described as owner of a privateer and merchant, and resided at 1 Hood Street, St. Johns. While he was a captain he was a member of that "Liverpool Fireside," whose minutes have been preserved from 1776 to 1781. From this we find he was born 12th July, though in what year "deponent sayeth not." On 25th January 1802, "Ellen Fairweather, widow of the late Captain Patrick Fairweather (of 1 Hood Street, St. Johns), gives notice that she has removed to 1 Shaw's Place or Haymarket, where she has genteel accommodation for board and lodging." By 1805 she had opened premises at 45 King Street as a tea-dealer and hosier. By 1811 she had a similar business at 34 Ranelagh Street, and here she was in 1818, when the name of her son appears at the same address as "banker." She was still at that number in 1821, but her son had taken separate premises at 60 Ranelagh Street. But by 1823 they were both at 2 Cases Street, she as tea-dealer and hosier, and he as banker. But by 1825 he, as above stated, is no longer a banker. The crisis in the ever memorable year of 1825 doubtless put an end to his venture, though no trace of his name has been found among those who went down.   Ellen Fairweather died on 5th October of the same year, aged 76 years.

Robert Fairweather after her death resided for a while at Orrell, and died at his house in Everton Crescent on 26th February 1828, aged 41 years.

CHAPTER XXII

MERSEY BANK.

OF the fraudulent character of this bank there
can be no doubt. It was simply created to foist
worthless paper on the public, and, but for the
vigilance and plucky perseverance of Egerton
Smith, might have succeeded to a greater extent
than it did. In Aris's Birmingham paper of 7th
May 1821 appears a story to the effect that an
engraver had been employed by a firm professing
to trade under the name of the "Mersey Bank"
to prepare notes for £1 and £5, and bills for £15.
The plates were completed, and handed to the
employer, who decamped without paying for
them. They purport to be drawn on Messrs.
Willerton, Beaumont, Graham, & Co., Bankers,
Waterloo Place, Pall Mall, London, by Morton,
Hardie, Walker, & Smyth, of the Mersey Bank.

In May 1821 the *Morning Chronicle* published

a notice to the effect that an attempt had
been made to bring off a huge swindle in
Liverpool.

On 12th May 1821 D. Andrews was brought
up at the Guildhall charged with extensive fraud.
He intended, in collusion with others, to found a
fraudulent bank under the name of the Mersey
Bank, introducing two or three names of well-
known respectability intermixed with those of
persons whose intention it was to commit one of
the most mischievous and ruinous frauds that was,
perhaps, ever practised. Notes to the nominal
amount of many thousands of pounds were produced, with the signatures cut off. The parties,
having had some intimation that the fraud was discovered, did this to prevent a charge of forgery.
The prisoner was discharged on account of no evidence being produced that any of these notes had
been put into circulation. The *Liverpool Mercury*
published all the above, and its then editor and
proprietor, Egerton Smith, was very keen on
obtaining and retailing all information on the
subject, and to the columns of the *Mercury* I am
indebted for all the facts of this paper. The so-
called bank had opened a place of business in
Church Street, with the name "Mersey Bank"
painted thereon, and they at once issued two
writs on the *Liverpool Mercury* for publication of
the above facts. Mr. Johnson Gore, of Gore's

Advertiser, was also served with a writ. The wording of one of the writs on the *Mercury* ran that they " broke into the close of the said bankers with force of arms, and that they did other wrongs to the great damage of Daniel Worton, James Hardie, and Wm. Smyth." The *Mercury* treated the matter with great contempt, and said that if ever they break into a bank, they will do so into one in which they expect to find something. The editor could not restrain his characteristic love for puns, and sent the following to the boy in charge of the bank, to be by him presented to his masters, *if he can find them* :—

> "Great sirs, it bankers ill befits
> Instead of bills to issue writs !
> So drop your suit without delay ;
> O Mersey Bank ! have mercy, pray ! "

Early in December of the said year Egerton Smith cautions his readers, while referring to the Mersey Bank, against bill forgeries of an extensive description, bearing apparent endorsements of respectable houses at Manchester, Halifax, and Huddersfield. The bearing of this observation was evident later, when John Duckworth in December 1821 was committed to the Lancaster Assizes for negotiating a forged bill of exchange. As the evidence brought out the character and standing of the Mersey Bank, a précis is given of what was stated at the trial. The prisoner, John Duckworth, had called on one Jonathan Ball, tobacconist, Whitechapel, Liverpool, stating that he was a tobacconist in Chorlton Row, Manchester, and purchased £50 worth of tobacco. He paid for it by a bill of exchange bearing the endorsement of Shakespeare G. Sikes, banker, Huddersfield, which, together with the bill, was found to be a forgery. The prisoner was apprehended at Coventry. William Hide Sikes was also committed at the same time for passing forged bills. A bill for £125, drawn by Thomas Hogg & Co. of Holbeck, near Leeds, and having the endorsement of Rawdon Briggs and Co., William Bates & Co., and Shakespeare G. Sikes, was presented at the bank of Messrs. Lowry, Roscoe, & Wardell of Liverpool for discount by a Mr. Matthew Samuel Haynes of 15 Blake Street, and who stated he had received it in a letter from Leeds. Messrs. Lowry and Co., having found the bill to be a forgery, sent to Mr. Haynes' lodgings, and were there referred to the "Mersey Bank," in Church Street, of which concern Mr. Haynes was found to be the corresponding clerk. After some difficulty they succeeded in getting from him £17, 1s., which he said was the *whole of the money then in the bank*. They were then referred by Mr. Haynes to a Mr. [John] Richardson of

14 Upper Newington, who was stated to be the cashier to the "Mersey Bank," and from him they received two bills, one of £20, and the other of £30 (which bills Lowry & Co. had previously paid to Mr. Haynes), and the balance of the £125 in a draft on London. It appeared from the testimony of Haynes that the prisoner Sikes presented the bill to the Mersey Bank for discount, and there had it discounted in *local notes of their own*, with the exception of £30 in cash. On the day of the discovery of the forgery Sikes sent a bill to the Mersey Bank to be discounted for £98, 16s., drawn by John Milnes, Huddersfield, on William Dickinson, Ironmonger Lane, London, accepted at Masterman's, and endorsed George Clay and Shakespeare G. Sikes.

Then a mythical person, John Peacock, writing from 40 Wapping, Liverpool, to the *Dublin Morning Post*, denies the accuracy of the above account which had appeared in the *Liverpool Mercury*. He states that the *Mercury* had offered £1000 and all expenses to Messrs. Worton, Hardie, & Co. to compromise the action of libel which the latter were bringing against the former. Whereon the *Mercury* waxes wroth, denies that they ever offered 1000 farthings, much less £1000, to Worton and Co.; it inquires who the latter are, states that it cannot trace them in any way, although the "bank" in Church Street is decorated with their names, and says that they verily believe that there are no such persons in existence. It also wants to know who Mr. Peacock is, and asks for some reference, banker, merchant, or tradesman, who can vouch for his respectability.

Then the *Mercury* on 11th January 1822 became even more outspoken. "The opinion we formed as to the character and views of the projectors of the 'Mersey Bank' has been too fully confirmed. . . . We do not speak on light grounds when we pronounce the Mersey Bank is, what we have all along regarded it to be, INSOLVENT. There are now in this town, both in the hands of bankers and other persons, several of their bills protested for non-payment. Their small notes for £5, and even those for £1, have been dishonoured." There are several communications from correspondents. One presented two of the notes for £1 each to Willerton & Co., Waterloo Place, and was refused payment. The reason assigned was that the house at Liverpool had overdrawn; but they Willerton's) are in daily expectation of a remittance. A jocular correspondent writes that although the house seemed to be blown upon, yet their paper goes farther than that of any other Liverpool banker. The bills of the latter go to London and stop

there, a distance of 200 miles, while those of
the former go to London, and invariably come
back. Hence the bills of the Mersey Bank go
twice as far as those of any other Liverpool
bank.

On 21st January 1822 the following circular
was issued :—

"MERSEY BANK, LIVERPOOL.

"Messrs. Worton, Hardie, & Co. having been under
the necessity (from concurrent circumstances which
they could not control) to suspend the payment of
their engagements, respectfully announce to the several
holders of their notes and bills that all their notes on
demand will be paid in the months of February and
March—viz. all the £1 notes in the last week of
February and the second week of March, and the £5
notes in the last week of March and the second week of
April, during which time an arrangement will be made
for paying all bills after sight or date. Interim they
request, wherever it can be done, the holders of such
bills will return them to the parties to whom they were
issued."

The *Gazette* for 18th February contains a
notice of dissolution of partnership of D.
Worton, James Hardie, W. Walker, and William
Smyth of Liverpool, bankers.

The *Mercury* for 1st February 1822 says:
"*Mersey Bank.*—This respectable body have, for
the present, retired from the fatigues of business,
. . . as they have declined in favour of *John Doe*

and *Richard Roe*, who have present possession of the bank in Church Street."

The cashier of the Mersey Bank was called as a witness in a forgery case in the next April, and in reply to questions said that of the four partners of the Mersey Bank, two he had never seen, Walker and Smyth.   Daniel Worton resided at Little Chelsea, and William Smyth at Pall Mall. None of them resided in Liverpool.

In May, in a case of insolvent debtors, it was stated in Court that none of the partners of the Mersey Bank or Waterloo Bank could be found. In October one of the notes of the Mersey Bank on Willerton, Beaumont, & Graham was returned to Newcastle with answer, "No such firm in existence."

In November 1822 Thomas Ambrose applied for his discharge in the Insolvent Debtors Court. He had been discharged about two and a half years ago from debts to the amount of £7000. Six months after his discharge he took the house in Waterloo Place, Pall Mall, from where the Waterloo Bank was carried on.   The insolvent was an anonymous partner in the bank.   There was such a person as Willerton in existence.   He formerly lived at Pontefract, and now resides at Hull.   There was also a person named Beaumont. He formerly resided at Islington, but his present residence is unknown.   Bills were drawn in the

name of D. Miaston, but no person of that name
had to do with the bank.   Asked if a bill drawn
in that name was not in his handwriting, insolvent
appealed to the Court that he was not bound to
answer.   Discharge refused.

INDEX

Roscoe, Edward, 70
—— Henry, 71
—— Sir Henry, 71, 80
—— James, 70
—— Margaret, 70
—— Margaret, 70
—— Mary Anne, 71
—— Richard, 71
—— William, 4, 53, 57, 59–61, 81–3, 191
—— William Caldwell, 81
—— William Stanley, 63, 68, 76–81
Ryle, John C., 90 n.

SANDBACH, Gilbert R., 47
—— Samuel, 47
Serjeantson, Elizabeth, 99
—— William, 99
Shaw, Ellen, 57
Shepherd, Dr. William, 58
Sheridan, Richard B., 88
—— Thomas, 88
Sitwell, Alice, 115
—— Francis, 115
—— Sir George, Bart., 115
—— Sir Sitwell, Bart., 115
Slaves and slavery, 4, 63 n., 133, 141, 171, 200, 212
Smith, Egerton, 224–5
—— J. B., 207 n.
—— James, 161 n.
—— James, & Son, 161 n.
Smyth, Edward, 88, 89
—— Thomas, 84–9
—— Rev. Thomas, 88
—— William, 223, 225, 229, 230
—— Prof. William, 87, 88, 177
Smythe, Ann, 115
—— John Groome, 115
Sovereigns and half-sovereigns, 22, 23, 43
Speculations, 19, 25–7
Staniforth, Ingram, Bold, & Daltera, 127–43
—— Samuel, 129–30
—— Sarah, 131 n.

Staniforth, Thomas, 127–9
—— Rev. Thomas, 130, 130 n., 131 n.
Stanyforth, E. W., 131 n.
Statham, Richard, 146, 148
Steer, Catharine, 134
Stonehouse, James, 204
Stringer, James, 73 n.
Stuart, Miss, 168
Syers, Robert, 207

TARLETON, Banastre, 62
—— Clayton, 144, 146
—— John, 76–8, 80
—— John, M.P., 153 n.
—— Thomas, 196, 210 n.
Taylor, Hannah, 192
—— Moss, & Co., 190
—— Thomas, 192
Thompson, Arthur, 101 n.
—— Elizabeth, 101
—— Frances C., 101 n.
—— Henry Yates, 103 n.
—— James, Jun., 101 n.
—— Samuel, 97, 99, 100, 140
—— Samuel Henry, 101, 103
—— William, Jun., 101 n.
—— Yates, Rev. S. A., 103 n.
Threlfall, Alice, 219
—— John, 217–19
—— John Mayor, 218–19
Threlfall's Brewery Co. Ltd., 219
Tooke, Thomas, 26, 27
Town's meetings, 20–2, 31, 144–6
Troughton, Richard, 1
—— Richard, 211
—— Susan, 211

UNIVERSITY OF LIVERPOOL, 82, 103 n., 209 n.
Usury Acts, 45

"VILLAGE BLACKSMITH," 160 n.

VOLUNTEERS, 130 n., 132, 139
—— dress of, 132

INDEX

343

Printed by BALLANTYNE, HANSON & Co.
Edinburgh & London

HENRY YOUNG & SONS' PUBLICATIONS

CHARACTER AND CONDUCT. A Book of Helpful Thoughts, by Great Writers of Past and Present Ages, selected and arranged for Daily Reading by the Author of "Being and Doing." Illustrated with a Collotype Frontispiece of the picture, "Faithful unto Death," by Sir E. J. POYNTER, Bart., P.R.A., reproduced by permission of the Liverpool Corporation. Crown 8vo, cloth extra, 3s. 6d. net. Also in various leather bindings, from 6s. net to 12s. 6d. net

Third impression, sixth thousand, of this admirable and stimulating book. It is the author's best work, and should be in the possession of all persons wishing to strengthen their character by communing with the greatest thoughts of the greatest and wisest men and women.

COLE (S.). First Impressions of Florence. Illustrated with Plates in Colour. 8vo, cloth extra, top edge gilt, 7s. 6d. net.

Privately printed, and only a few copies for sale.

LIVERPOOL BANKS AND BANKERS, 1760-1837. By JOHN HUGHES. Illustrated with 25 Fine Plates, consisting of Portraits of Eminent Bankers, and views of ancient Bank premises, Facsimiles of Local Bank Notes, and a Coloured Frontispiece; nicely printed on fine paper. Small 8vo, cloth, 7s. 6d. net. Idem, on Large Paper, limited to 100 copies, each signed by the author, printed on hand-made paper, half bound in leather, gilt top, 4to, 21s. net.

LIVERPOOL IN KING CHARLES THE SECOND'S TIME, written in the year 1667-8. By Sir EDWARD MOORE, Bart. Edited from the original MS. by W. FERGUSSON IRVINE, F.S.A., with a Preface, Historical Introduction, and Notes. Illustrated with fine Photogravure Plates, Plans, and Maps. 4to, cloth, top edge gilt, 21s. net.

The most ancient description of Liverpool and its early inhabitants known. It contains a complete list of the people paying the HEARTH TAX in 1663, which has never been printed before, and which virtually forms the Earliest Known Liverpool Directory —older by more than 100 years than Gore's first Directory. Only 250 copies have been printed, and no more will be published.

CAROË (W. D.) AND GORDON (E. J.). Descriptive and Historical Account of Sefton and Sefton Church, Lancashire, comprising the Collected Notes and Researches of the late Rev. E. HORLEY. Numerous Plates. Royal 8vo, white buckram extra, 10s. 6d. (pub. 30s. net.)

Sefton Church dates from the 14th century, and is the richest in point of ancient decoration in the neighbourhood of Liverpool.

GAMLIN (MRS. H.). 'Twixt Mersey and Dee; a Guide to the Principal Villages, Hamlets, Antiquities, Churches, Ancient Residences, &c., of the Hundred of Wirral, interspersed with Local Histories, and Illustrated with numerous Plates, including a Coloured Frontispiece of Birkenhead Ferry in 1845, and a copy of the Survey of the river Dee, from Chester to its mouth, made in 1684-89, showing the course, depth of water, sandbanks, &c. Crown 8vo, cloth, 5s. net.

IRVINE (W. FERGUSSON, F.S.A.). Notes on the Old Halls of Wirral. Illustrated with views of Shotwick, Poole, and Irby. Printed upon hand-made paper, and bound in white buckram, top edge gilt, 8vo, 3s. 6d. net.

Only 400 copies printed, and the type distributed.

LIVERPOOL: HENRY YOUNG & SONS, 12 SOUTH CASTLE STREET

HENRY YOUNG & SONS' PUBLICATIONS

IRVINE (W. FERGUSSON, F.S.A.). Notes on the Parish Churches of Wirral. Frontispiece View of Bebington Church. Printed upon hand-made paper and bound in white buckram, top edge gilt.

IRVINE (W. FERGUSSON, F.S.A.) and BEAZLEY (F. C.). Notes on the Parish of Woodchurch. Illustrated with 3 Plates. 8vo, paper covers, 2s. net.

IRVINE (W. FERGUSSON, F.S.A.). Notes on Hall I' Th' Wood, Bolton, Lancashire, and its Owners. Illustrated with a Plan and five Views of the Hall, in 1825, 1858, and 1904, also an Engraving of the South Staircase. Printed upon hand-made paper, with silver-grey paper covers, 8vo, 2s. 6d. net, or in white buckram, 3s. 6d. net.
Only 200 copies printed, and the type distributed.

THE CHESHIRE SHEAF. Being Local Gleanings, Historical and Antiquarian, relating to Cheshire, Chester, and North Wales. Edited by Rev. F. SANDERS, W. FERGUSSON IRVINE, F.S.A., and J. BROWNBILL. Third series. Vols. 3, 4, and 5. 4to, paper covers, 6s. each net.

WIRRAL NOTES AND QUERIES. Being Local Gleanings, Historical and Antiquarian, relating to the Hundred of Wirral. Edited by Rev. F. SANDERS and W. FERGUSSON IRVINE, F.S.A. 2 Vols. 4to, paper covers, 15s. net.

FARRER (W.). The Lancashire Pipe Rolls and Early Lancashire Charters of the 11th and 12th Centuries, relating to the Honour and County of Lancaster. With a Coloured Map of Lancashire, indicating the Feudal Divisions, Tenure of each Township and Parochial Division as they existed at the time of the Great Inquest, taken at Midsummer, A.D. 1212. Royal 8vo, cloth, 21s. net.
Only 240 copies have been printed, and no more will be printed. The map is a most valuable feature, and is not to be seen in any other work.

FARRER (W.). History of the Parish of North Meols [Southport], in the Hundred of West Derby, with Historical and Descriptive Notices of Birkdale and Martin Mere. Illustrated with a fine Portrait of the Rev. Charles Hesketh, Pedigrees of the Coudray, Aughton, and Hesketh families, and 10 Plates, consisting of Maps of Southport and District in 1786, 1825, 1834, armorial bearings, &c. 4to, full bound in buckram, 21s. net. Large Paper issue, only 15 copies printed, royal 4to, full bound in buckram, £2, 10s. net.

HARRISON (H.). The Place Names of the Liverpool District, or the History and Meaning of the Local and River Names of South-West Lancashire, and of Wirral. Crown 8vo, cloth, 2s. 6d. net. Idem, on Large Paper, only 50 copies printed, 4to, cloth, 8s. 6d. net.
Interesting to all who desire to know the meaning of the names of places in this part of Lancashire and Cheshire, and how those names came to be attached to the places.

PLUTARCH'S LIVES OF EMINENT GREEKS AND ROMANS. The Translation called DRYDEN'S, corrected from the Greek and revised by A. H. CLOUGH. 5 Vols., nicely printed in large type, and illustrated with 5 pretty Photogravures. Cloth, top edges gilt, 30s. net. Also handsomely half bound in crimson levant morocco, crushed and polished, top edges gilt, £4 net.

WILLIE WEE'S ARM-CHAIR AND OTHER STORIES. A Book for Children. Crown 8vo, cloth, 2s. 6d. net.

LIVERPOOL : HENRY YOUNG & SONS, 12 SOUTH CASTLE STREET

Lightning Source UK Ltd.
Milton Keynes UK
UKHW010129200522
403272UK00002B/46